Dear Baby Girl,

Let the Adventures Begin

Jeanna Rangel

Fulton Books
Meadville, PA

Published by Fulton Books 2024

ISBN 979-8-89221-687-6 (paperback)
ISBN 979-8-89221-688-3 (digital)

Printed in the United States of America

January 23, 2002

Dear baby,

Today your daddy and I went to the doctor for an ultrasound, internal picture of you, and found out that you are a girl. It was exciting because I had been saying that you were a girl from the beginning. We were able to see you moving around inside of me. You were tossing and turning everywhere. It was hard for the nurse to take your picture because you were moving around so much. We did happen to get a few pictures though. We think that you're going to be tall just like your daddy. You have long skinny feet. I think you'll have your daddy's nose too.

While we were watching you on the screen, we were able to see your heartbeat and noticed that you had hiccups. You were just so cute and so alive inside me. It was amazing to see you moving on the screen, but I couldn't feel your movements inside me yet.

I've been reading a lot of baby books lately, and one of them touched on feelings that women might have while they were becoming a mother. I've been experiencing mixed feelings about becoming a mother. Not that I don't want you or wouldn't love you, but I've been feeling sad, anxious, scared, loving…just to name the strongest ones.

I'm sad that I have no control over what being pregnant does to my body. I'm five months pregnant with you, and I'm still getting morning sickness. It can be frustrating to not be in control of your own body.

Anxious to have you in my life. I'm anticipating the love I will have for you when you finally come out into the world, where I can hold you in my arms and kiss your little fingers, toes, and face. I'm ready to be a mother. I'm ready to be your mother.

Scared of the new life changes of being a parent. Will I be a good mom and be able to provide you with what you will need? I'm scared of making mistakes. Although, mistakes are okay. I just know that I will learn a lot from you.

I haven't seen you, and I have so much love for you that I'm excited to meet you. Every time I think of you, I want to cry tears of joy. My heart beats faster, and my breath gets weaker.

No matter what mistakes I make, I know that I will always love you. No matter what our future may bring our way. Thank you, baby, for listening and understanding this someday.

Love always,
Your Mommy

June 27, 2002

Dear Kendall May,

Being a mother is so unbelievable. You are now nineteen days old and as beautiful as ever. Everyone has told me that I would forget the pain of pregnancy, birth, and breastfeeding when I would see you in my arms because it would all be worth it. I don't think I'll forget the pain, but you are worth it.

I melt when I hold you in my arms. My eyes get all teary when I look at your dark blue eyes and soft sweet face. I feel pain in my heart when you cry. I never knew that I could ever feel so much love for someone as much as I do you.

It feels different having a daughter. It's hard to believe that you are a part of me. You have my eyebrows, lips, a chin, and a facial shape. I think you'll have my attitude. There are times you cry because you don't want to be touched. You don't like to be smothered with attention.

I'm still nervous about taking you out in public. I don't have enough confidence in myself. Being a mom isn't easy. I have so much more respect for my mother now. I understand her a lot more.

You fall asleep with your face against my chest. When we take naps together, you curl up next to me and snuggle. You know my smell and comfort as well as when I get frustrated. You can feel my emotions like you're reading them from a book.

You are so perfect. Everyone thinks you're the cutest baby, and I agree. I'm so glad that you're my daughter. I couldn't have asked for a more perfect baby than you are. Thank you for selecting me as your mother. At least one of us has confidence in me being a parent.

I promise you that I'm going to try to be a good mom. I warn you now; I will make mistakes, so please try to understand. I love you with all my heart.

Love always,
Mom

August 8, 2002

Dear Kendall,

It is a week before you're three months old. You have changed so much since the last time I wrote. You smile all the time now, not just after you eat any more. You've laughed a couple of times now, not really understanding what it is that you're doing when you do laugh.

You're talking a lot more. More nonsense and cooing, not real words. Daddy talks to you in Spanish, and your face lights up. You even talk back to him when he talks to you in Spanish.

You're recognizing faces. You know Mommy, Daddy and Grandma Rice's faces and voices. You follow us with your eyes. When we walk away, your eyes follow. It's so cute. You are so cute.

You are normally a great baby. The only time you really cry is when you're hungry, tired, or you have gas from something I ate that your tummy didn't agree with. Yesterday was the first time I left you alone with Daddy. I went shopping, and you stayed home with Daddy. You were very good until I came home and you heard my voice. You started screaming uncontrollably and loud. As soon as I started to breastfeed you, you stopped. I don't know if it was because you missed me or because you were hungry.

Today you were acting differently. It felt as though you had colic. You were crying hysterically and uncontrollably for over an hour. I tried feeding you, changing your diaper, rocking you. I gave you Tylenol and gas relief. Nothing. The only thing that would stop you from crying was to hold you in my arms with your tummy facing the floor and rocking you. You wouldn't even let me sit down or you would start crying again. Finally, after you calmed down, I tried feeding you again. You fell asleep in the middle of eating. You were completely worn out from crying so much. You wore me out too.

I'm glad that you went to sleep. I was getting frustrated. I was scared because I didn't know what you were crying so hard about. I hate to see you cry so hard. Your eyes were red, and tears were pouring out. It breaks my heart to see you cry so hard.

I love you so much. I really don't want to leave you and go back to work. I don't want to leave you with someone else, but we can't afford for me to stay home. I wish I could.

Just remember, no matter how frustrated Mommy gets, I will always love you.

Love always,
Mommy

October 17, 2002

Dear Kendall,

Where do I begin? I love you so much. You <u>are</u> the cutest baby. I'm not just saying that because I'm your mother either. Everywhere you go, someone tells you that you're the cutest baby. Mom's friend Crystal Hissam tells people that you look like a porcelain doll.

You don't really like your Binky to suck on anymore. Now you just play with it. You wrap the string around your thumb and suck on that. You're starting to stick more things in your mouth. You suck on your tongue or try to. You also suck on your bottom lip. You make noise and get frustrated with your bottom lip like you're mad at it. It makes me laugh when I watch you.

You still haven't started crawling, but somehow, you maneuver your way around on your back. A week or two ago, I put you on the floor lying on your back with your toy gym. I was in the kitchen making dinner. I came out to check on you, and you managed to get all the way under the couch. Even your head was covered. It was like you were talking to the couch. You were mumbling to the couch and squealing. I took a picture of you. I was cracking up.

I took you out to Bonnie's yesterday while I was going to work. I cried from Bonnie's all the way to work. I hate giving you to someone else to watch you. I'd rather be at home with you. I hate being away from you all day. I only get to see you for a couple of hours or so a day, and I wish it was more.

You're starting to really recognize me now when I pick you up from Bonnie's and Grandma's. You light up and smile when you see me. It makes me feel so good. My heart melts when I see you. I take you into my arms and squeeze you and kiss you all over. I sure do miss seeing you all day. You are the best part of my days.

I miss taking naps with you in my arms and cuddling. I'm afraid now that you'd move yourself off the bed if I were not paying attention. You're so sweet when you sleep.

I still can't believe that you're four months old. You're growing so fast. I love you very much.

Love,
Mom

December 2002

Dear friends and family,

Well, it's that time of year again. I hope that everyone is doing well. Everyone grows so fast. I receive pictures of cousins and friends that I hardly recognize. Having a baby really makes time go by fast.

We're doing well. We're not living with Grandma anymore. We got our own place in September, but we have the same mailing address. I am not working right now. I decided to quit my job and be a full-time mom for now until I find something else that I want to do. I love being a mom. I really feel that this is the best job I've ever had.

Kendall just turned six months this month, and at times she still seems so small, and then she'll do something major like roll over or sit up on her own. She laughs a lot and smiles all the time. I love getting up in the morning now just to see her smiling face. She's really starting to figure out who everyone is and it's cute. She lights up when Art talks to her in Spanish. He's a very good dad to her. They really enjoy each other when they get the chance. She is the best baby too! She's been sleeping through the night since she was two or three months old and is only fussy when she's either hungry or tired. Even then she's not fussy. We're starting to feed her cereal and pureed food. She loves peaches!

Art is doing great! He's working for a trail position for the county. He's working as a social worker helping mentally ill people. He loves his job and finds it very rewarding. He's using his brain a lot more now, and so he comes home with headaches. He's still taking classes, but now he's taking classes to better himself in his job. He just finished a counseling class and is taking Sociology and Physical, Chemical, and Behavioral Effects of Alcohol and Drugs. He's learning more every day. He was also mentioned in the Lake Tahoe Community College schedule of classes this quarter. I'm very proud of him!

Grandma is doing well. She still has her boyfriend from New York. She just recently dyed her hair, and now she has no gray. It looks good! She looks so much younger now. It's amazing what a little coloring can do. She's working at the same place. Loves being a grandmother! She shows Kendall off to everyone wherever we go somewhere. People think that Kendall is sometimes her daughter because of the way she carries on. It's funny. She seems so much younger now. She has more energy than she used to.

I hope that everyone is doing great. We wish you all well. Happy holidays to all!

Love,
Jeanna, Arturo, and Kendall Rangel

PS: This is not Kendall on the front of this card, but it does look like her, and that's why I got them.

January 8, 2003

Dear Kendall,

Today you are seven months old. You sure are growing fast. Sometimes I feel as though I've taken for granted the fact that I'm around you all day long. I've been a stay-at-home mom for a little over a month and have the advantage of seeing you all day long. I love it! I love being able to spend quality time with you. I can't wait until summer. You really enjoy being outside. We'll go to the beach, go for walks, and play in the parks.

I enjoy playing with you. That is, when you let me. You're becoming more independent and like to play by yourself more often. It's good in some sense because I don't have to give you so much attention. I can cook dinner without having to hold you so much, but now you're crawling, and I must keep a closer eye on you. And you're fast! I usually put you in your walker in the kitchen with me.

I'm getting the feeling that you don't need me as much. I miss that you depend on me all the time for everything. You don't like me to rock you to sleep anymore. You like your crib more. You move around in your sleep a lot. I put you in the crib face up in the middle of the mattress. When I go to check on you, you're on your stomach in the corner of the crib. You like to go to bed with your stuffed Piglet toy. You always have it close by your side when you're sleeping. I can't take naps with you anymore either. You like your own space. I miss holding you in my arms while you lay your head on my chest to sleep.

You're developing an attitude now. You get mad about something, and you grunt or scream. Making your arms stiff by your sides, and I can't help but to laugh because it's so funny. You're starting to pinch when you get mad too. I don't like that though. You pinch hard.

You used to let anyone hold you. Now you're getting picky. You cried the other day when Uncle Jeff said hi to you. You cried when I put you on Grandma Helen's lap. You cry when I walk in a room and don't pick you up after I've been away for a while. You smile when you see me walk in the room. That, in return, makes me smile.

You smile when your daddy comes home from work because you haven't seen him all day. You still love listening to your daddy talk to you in Spanish. When he's on the phone, your head turns to wherever you hear his voice. You love playing peekaboo with him too. He's a pretty good daddy to you. He loves you very much too.

You started eating baby food a little before you turned six months old, and you've been doing very well. I started giving you one new item at a time, just to see how you'd do. You like everything. The vegetables must be warmed up though. I usually give you half a jar of vegetables and half a jar of fruit. You love your sippy cup.

You started making fish lips one day on your own. I don't think anyone ever showed you how to do it. You don't really kiss yet, but when someone asks you for a kiss, you move your face towards the person.

I got you some smelly toys, an apple, and a peanut butter and jelly sandwich. When I tell you to smell and show you how to do it, you copy me and smell them.

Someone at the store last night said that you were so beautiful. She said that you looked like a porcelain doll. People tell me that all the time. That makes me feel so good when people tell me things like that about you. They also tell me what a good baby you are. I am proud to be your mom. You are beautiful, and I love you very much. I hope that while you grow up, you will always need me. I hope that we have a close relationship forever. I like being needed because I need you.

Love you always,
Mom

January 30, 2003

Dear Kendall,

It's my twenty-sixth birthday today. Hard to believe that you've been a part of my life for a year and four months. When I was younger, I had planned on being married with a baby by the time I was twenty-five years old, but I didn't know if it would happen or not. I love my little family.

I was so excited yesterday. You were saying ma-ma all day long. It was really the first time you said it more than once. It made me feel so good. You even started sitting up on your hands and knees and rocking. You just did it all on your own. You only did it a few times, but still, that was an accomplishment.

Last night, we went to a social group get-together, and people were holding and playing with you. You didn't even fuss. You like being around crowds of people. You've become quite the social butterfly. You're even sick with a cold, and you weren't even cranky.

Yesterday was our first meeting with our home visit teacher, Stacia. She had me fill out a form about where you were as far as development. You were above where you needed to be, and you're only seven and a half months old. We put Cheerios in front of you to see if you could pick them up, and you did it all on your own.

Today you've been crawling in and out of the bottom of your walker. Occasionally, you get stuck and frustrated, but you keep doing it. It's funny.

You make an *O* shape with your lips. I'm trying to get you to make the sound with it as well. You copied me once today.

During the Super Bowl XXXVII, there was this commercial on TV where the dad was watching a football game with his four-year-old son. The boy was putting his arms in the air and saying, "Touchdown." We taught you the same thing. After the Super Bowl was over, I was trying to change it to "Kendall's a big girl." You do it on your own now and try to get someone else to do it with you.

You keep me going with something new all the time. I love you very much.

Love always,
Mom

February 27, 2003

Dear Kendall,

You're doing so much now. You're walking along the furniture and moving fast. You can walk from one thing to another. You do it so gracefully too. You are becoming so much more independent. You don't like to be held as much. You push your way around and swat things with your hands when you don't want something.

Grandma Rice bought you these toys where you can either walk behind them or ride on them. You love them! You try to walk so fast that you're almost running, and you get so excited about it. They're sort of like walkers.

You clap your hands with Daddy while he sings a song: "Chiquiti-boom-a-la-bin-bon-ban, chiquiti-boom-a-la-bin-bon-ban, a-la-vio-a-la-vao-a-la-bin-bon-ban, Kendal-Kendall-ra-ra-ra." Spanish, of course.

You're really climbing up the stairs. You try to do it by yourself. I was in the kitchen one day and came out to the living room to see what you were doing, and you were already on the third stair. You climb all the way to the top with no help, but we're usually behind you just in case you do fall. When it comes to going back down, you try to go down face-first. You haven't figured out how to go down backwards.

You get bored with just a bottle now. You want to eat more adult food. Tonight, I came to sit with you in the living room while I ate, and you played. You crawled over to me and tried to get the food off my plate. We will give you some of the food that we eat, but I'm afraid of allergies because you haven't tried a lot of things. You always let me know if you don't like something. You're not really excited about baby cereals. I'm not sure why.

You drink juice out of a sippy cup by yourself. Of course, it has a spill-proof lid so that you can't throw juice all over the house. You drank out of a straw the other night at dinner. We were very impressed.

You're also starting to wave hello/goodbye. We were at a restaurant one day, and you waved at another little girl three tables away.

You amaze me sometimes with the things you do. You're growing up so fast. I just started back to work full time. I think it's harder for me to be away from you all day. When I leave in the morning, you're OK. When I come home, you light up, but it takes a few minutes before I hold you, or you start crying. You don't cry very long before you want to go back to playing. I hate being away from you for a long period. I miss you. When I pick you up, you're tired. You're almost ready for bed when we get home. I'm afraid I'll miss out on some new achievements you've made.

You crawl on your hands and knees. You move faster than you used to.

You have two front teeth on the bottom that have come in. You're doing well with the teething thing. Every now and then, we must give a couple of teething tablets for the pain.

I've cut your bangs and hair three times now. Your hair grows so fast. Your hair starts to cover your eyes, and then I cut it.

You have a play telephone that I bought you. I'll pick up the receiver and say hello. I hand it to you. You hold the receiver to your ear and make a noise like you're trying to say hello. You try to mimic the sounds. You make me laugh all the time with the things that you do. I love watching you grow up. You're going to be so independent and beautiful, not to mention smart. I love you very much.

Love,
Mom

April 22, 2003

Dear Kendall,

You're doing so much now. You started walking and became a walkin' mama over the weekend. You don't want to be held anymore. You just want to walk all the time. One night, Daddy and I were having you walk back and forth to one another. On one turn to Daddy, you let go of my hand, turned, and ran into the wall face-first. I know that it hurt at the time, but it was so funny. Daddy and I were crackin' up.

Since you've been walking, you've had more than a couple of bruises, running into things, and bruising your head. I guess it comes with learning to walk. You're getting your fourth tooth in.

You're eating more and more adult food. You really like bananas and rice. You like eating with everyone else. You're not quite feeding yourself with a spoon just yet. You can drink from a straw though. Most children don't accomplish the straw until after two years old.

You're very smart. We've shown you how to put shaped blocks into the correct holes a couple of times, and then you do it yourself.

When I ask you, "What does a puppy say?" You say, "Woof."

"What does a kitty say?"

"Eow."

You clap your hands when we say, "Applaud."

You blink your eyes when Daddy says, "Ojitos."

We all went to Sebastopol, California, to visit the McCarns for Easter, and I put you in this cute little pink dress that your Abuelita gave to you. You were the talk of the party. Everyone thought you were so cute. I was so proud to say that you are our daughter. You are so beautiful. I am very proud of you. You were so well-behaved. You really are a good baby. The only time you really fuss is when you want or don't want something, when you're hungry or tired. Of course, there are days when you're being a brat, but it's not very often.

You're starting to kiss and hug for goodbyes. The other day, you wouldn't let me leave until you gave me a hug. Three of them. It was so cute. I love you so much. That started my day off great.

Love,
Mom

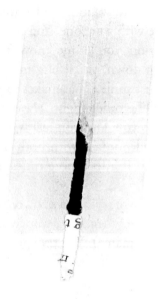

June 3, 2003

Dear Kendall,

I can hardly believe that in just five days, you'll be one year old. I'm excited! Watching you grow and develop into a beautiful little girl has been so joyous! I'm glad that you are part of our lives.

You're walking and mumbling like you're always going somewhere with someone. You play by yourself a lot, but when you want attention, you let me know. You come up and grab my leg, or if I'm sitting down, you'll hug me. You wrap your little arms around me and just smile. That makes me feel so special. I love that.

The other night, I was trying to put you to sleep lying down next to you, and you just weren't ready. You sat up, leaned over, and grabbed my face with both hands and kissed me. I got teary-eyed. You did it a few more times. It was so cute. My heart melted with love.

You're trying to say words now. You're saying sounds like kiddy (kitty), eow (meow), woo woo (woof), aua (agua), da da (daddy), ma ma (mama). You try hard. You even move your mouth to try and copy words, but sometimes no sound comes out. It's like a mime that mimics.

You really like being around other kids close to your age. When we were in Los Angeles a week ago, you played with your cousins Chelita, Andres, and Aaron. You were running back and forth from one room to another, just smiling and laughing. When there are kids around, you get excited.

You haven't been eating as much food. You're spitting food out and refusing to eat. You'll take bottles though, so I'm not too worried. At least you're eating.

You are becoming quite the monkey. You're climbing on things. Yesterday at Grandma's, you were standing on the couch and trying to pull yourself up onto the counter. You're strong too. This morning, you tried to climb out of your playpen to get a couple of balloons out. You can climb onto the couch now. Grandma told me that when

I was younger, I climbed on top of the refrigerator. I can hardly wait for that to happen to you.

I love you very much!

Love,
Mommy

July 13, 2003

Dear Kendall,

You are thirteen months old. You are so much fun. You want to play with Mom and Dad all the time. We're either chasing you around the house or lying on the floor so that you can climb on us like a jungle gym. You can climb on the couch yourself. You usually get a head start, run, and then swing your leg up to pull yourself onto the couch.

You're talking a little more. You can say "Me Me" for little me. You can say your vowels in Spanish: a, e, i, o, u. *Gatto* for kitty, and you make an "mmm: sound for cow or *baca*. When we ask you where your *pancita* is, you lift your shirt and show us your belly button. You copy Grandma Rice when she puts her hand over her mouth for surprise.

We just got the kitties that were at Grandma's house. You were so excited when you woke up the first day to find the kitties in your room. You chase them all over the house. You really like your kitties.

You're not drinking out of a bottle anymore, and I put you on Lactaid milk because you were getting a rash from whole milk. You got the allergy from me. You're picky about food. You spit out the food before you really taste it. Sometimes you spit milk, water, whatever out like a fountain because you think it's cute.

You're starting to go to bed by yourself more. You still have nights when Mommy must rock you to sleep, but not as long as it used to be.

When we read a book together, one we've read many times, you can point out some of the things in the book—butterfly, spider, Winnie Pooh.

When your Early Head Start teacher, Stacia, comes over, she usually brings a toy or something for you. This last week, she brought over a fold-up tunnel to crawl through. You didn't like it. You were playing with some cups instead. I took the cups and threw them in the tunnel. You picked up the tunnel and turned it until the cups fell out the other end. You surprised both Stacia and me. You are very smart.

You give hugs and kisses. When I drop you off at Grandma's in the mornings, you must give me a big hug and kiss before I leave. It really starts my day off to a great start. I love you so much.

Love,
Mom

August 7, 2003

Dear Kendall,

Tomorrow you will be fourteen months old. You say and know so many things now. Each day you become smarter and amaze me. Daddy talks to you in Spanish all the time. You're learning more Spanish than English, probably because instead of speaking only English to you, I practice Spanish with you. You know where your *ojos* (eyes), *nariz* (nose), *boca* (mouth), *la lengua* (tongue), and *panzita* (belly button) are.

In English, you can say *bipitu* (bicycle), *purpe* (purple), *pider* (spider), *buttery* (butterfly), *peas* (please), *ber* (bear), and *appa* (apple), and you can say your vowels in both English and Spanish. This is what I can remember right now as I'm writing to you. You even say words you don't even know by just repeating what others say.

You get frustrated easier now. When you can't figure something out or you have a hard time reaching something, you get mad. You don't like help very much either. You are very independent.

You really like playing with Jasmine and April. Jasmine is your favorite though. You get excited when you see them. They are Bonnie's two girls. Bonnie is the one that watches you while Mommy, Daddy, and Grandma are at work. She's been watching you since I went back to work.

You're picky when it comes to food. Some days you like something, and the next day, you don't even want it close to you. I guess you'll eat when you're hungry.

You're very good at giving hugs. You put your head on my shoulder, put your arms around, and squeeze me. Sometimes you even pat my arm or back. I love it when you hug me. I love you. I love you very much.

Love,
Mommy

September 23, 2003

Dear May May,

You are just full of surprises. You just blow me away with something new all the time. Quite a bit has happened since the last time I wrote you a letter.

You went on a vacation with Daddy. Your Abuelita Navarro came up from Los Angeles, stayed with us a couple of days, and then drove back down to Los Angeles. You were down there for four days. You played with your cousins and visited family. You hardly noticed I was gone. It was hard for me at first, but it was nice to have some time for myself. I sure did miss you and Daddy though.

You're saying a bunch of new words: *parse* (purse), *put on* (put it back on), *I you* (I see you), *ogert* (yogurt), *ow* (ouch), *bess you* (bless you), *petsel* (pretzel), *shu* (shoe), *pato* (zapato), *achew* (auh chew), *too* (two), *free* (three), *foe* (four), *fi* (five), *si* (six), *evn* (seven), *aigh* (eight), *ni* (nine), *ten*, *dos*, *tres*, *quato* (quarto), *sino* (*cinco*), *sei* (*seis*), *seiti* (*seite*), *osho* (*ocho*), *nue* (*nueve*), *diz* (*diez*), *ready*, *peech* (peach), *podde* (potty), *tautchu* (thank you), *pretty* (pretty), *happie* (happy), *open beep*, *down*, *all done*, *all gone*, *goch you* (gotch you), *wu you* (love you), *tita* (Motitia), *meno* (menso), *bita* (Abuelita), *tia*, *Bon-ne* (Bonnie), April, *horsie*, *butrfry* (butterfly), *pider* (spider), *kiya* (calle), and *toes*.

This morning, you were playing with a box of Band-Aids. There was a pattern on one side and white on the other. You had taken them out of the box and spread them all out. When you gathered them up, you put them all facing the same way. It was amazing to me that you paid attention to the order they were in. If they were wrong, you turned it so that it was right. I think you are going to be organized like your Mommy. And Grandma and Great-Grandma. You're cursed. I'm sorry.

Every morning on our way to Grandma's house, I let you drive in the front seat with me. When we approach a stop sign, I make you look both ways for cars coming. Most of the time, I must turn your head the opposite way to look. This morning, you grabbed your own head and turned it. I was cracking up. I thought it was so funny.

You're more interested in books now. You've always liked looking at the pictures and turning the pages, but you listen when you're being read too. Your favorite book is *My Friend Lucky, a Love Story* by David Milgrim. You ask me to read it about five times before you get up. It's about opposites. A little boy and his dog, Lucky.

You walk around the house with your hat and purse. Sometimes you even put my shoes on and walk around in them. You like dressing up.

Grandma bought you a tricycle, but you can't reach the pedals. I caught you standing on the seat with no hands. The tricycle stays outside unless someone is in the room with you.

You and Daddy race. You both put your fingers on the ground. Daddy says, "En sus marcas, listos, fuera," and you both run. It is so cute.

You point to your head when Daddy asks you where your *cabello* is and your ears (*dido*).

You are very smart! I am so proud of you. I love you very much.

Love,
Mommy

November 2, 2003

Dear Boo,

The weather had been warm for months, until the day before Halloween. It was cold and windy. It snowed on Halloween day. The first real snow of the season.

It was hard to go trick-or-treating because of the snow. You were a giraffe. You looked so cute! It was a one-piece jumper with spots in a giraffe pattern. It had a tail and a head on the hood with a mane. I didn't think you were going to wear the hood because you really don't like things on your head, but you kept it on your head the whole night. Daddy and I took you to a little carnival. You won three goldfish by throwing plastic balls into jars of water. You did it by yourself too. Then we took you trick-or-treating to a few houses. You wanted to keep knocking on doors. We didn't stay out too long.

When we got home, there were kids on our block trick-or-treating. When someone knocked on our door, you would run over to see the kids in their costumes. You had fun. Daddy and I had fun just watching you have fun.

The next day, we put our snowsuits and boots on. We went outside to play in the fresh powdery snow. You were eating, kicking, eating, throwing, eating, and eating some more. I think you're going to be a snow baby. Every time we go outside, you must eat some snow. We were going to take you sledding, but it eventually got cold and windy.

We bought you some little high-heel dress-up shoes. We call them your princess shoes. You put them on and grab your purse, hat, your baby, and stroller and walk around the house parading. It's cute.

You still really like books. I read about five to ten books a night before you go to bed. I must start watching you more closely with them though. You're starting to rip the pages.

I can't even tell you how many new words you can say because there are so many. You repeat almost everything you hear. Now we must watch what we say in front of you. You can say *gamma*, *mamma*, and *Jasmine* now. Jasmine is so happy that you can say her name.

When you count in English, you miss numbers: 1, 2, 3, 4, 5, 8, 9, 10. You think it's so funny. You can say parts of your ABCs. Not very many though.

Daddy and I were playing around and tickling each other, and Daddy had me down on the floor. You started screaming and crying. You thought Daddy was hurting me, and it made you very upset. Daddy tried to pick you up to let you know that everything was okay, and you got mad at him. You were screaming and kicking. You reached for me and hugged me. I guess it frightened you. It was strange. You had never done that before.

I love you very much!

Love,
Mommy

December 27, 2003

Dear Kendall,

You are just so funny. The latest thing that you've done that's funny is, for some reason—I don't know where you learned it from—picking the lint from between your toes. You were sitting on the floor one day being quiet, and I looked over to see what you were doing and noticed you were picking lint out of your toes. I asked you what you were doing, and then you showed me the lint you picked. You started laughing. I told you that you had icky toes.

You also laugh when I'm changing your diaper, and you fart in my face. I will call you a tutor and pinch your butt.

You put your fingers in your ears and say, "Tan't hear you."

You're talking a lot. You talk more than the average toddler your age. I bought you a couple of CDs with children's songs on them. When we get in the car, you say, "Eio cd" and "Good morning." You can sing most of "Twinkle, Twinkle Little Star," "Old McDonald," "Good Morning," "Mary Had a Little Lamb," your ABCs, and "Happy Birthday" to May May. There's more, but I can't remember them right now. Daddy and I try to read you about five books a night before you go to sleep. You know both Spanish and English words. Sometimes I wonder where you get some of the words you do speak.

We adopted a new kitten last month. We named him Buddy. Abbey and Motita do not let you touch them and hold them very much, and this cat does. You hold him by his chest, sometimes by the neck, or he sits in your lap. You sit on the couch and hold out your arms. "Hold him." You always want to hold him, but only for a few seconds, and then you push him away. I decided to call him Buddy because he's become just that, your buddy. He likes to rub on you, but you don't like that very much and end up pushing him away. I help put him in your baby doll stroller, and you stroll him around the house, like he's your baby.

Daddy and I took you out sledding yesterday, and you had fun. I took you down the hill with me this one time, and we hit a little bump, which blew snow up and into our faces. When we got to the bottom, I turned you around to face me, and your face was covered. It was funny, but you got cold real fast. You would go down the hill with Daddy, but you ended up not going down far because you would both tip over. You really like eating the snow more than playing in it.

For Christmas, you received a shopping cart with play food and a little kitchenette set. You play with them a lot. You like the shopping cart because it plays music. It sings a song, "Let's Go Shopping," and it claps. You clap along with it. You got a wagon, lots of clothes, a couple of wooden puzzles, Little People circus town, musical toy radio, a new baby doll, and a few more books.

You're growing so fast!

I love you!

Love,
Mom

December 12, 2003

Dear friends and family,

'Tis the season to be jolly! Who is this so-called person named Jolly anyway?

It's Christmastime again and time for catching up on the latest in family affairs. Who's been traveling and where? Who has a new job this year? Not me! It's about time I kept more consistency in my career.

'Twas the night before Christmas, when all through the house, not a creature was stirring, not even a mouse. I don't know whose house this was, but in my house, cats were running up and down, chasing one another's tails. The stockings were hung by the chimney (what chimney?) with care, in hopes that St. Nicholas soon would be there. YIPEE!

I'm still working for a real estate office doing marketing. I LOVE it! Still can't buy a house yet though. Housing here is so expensive. I just got over the horrible ten-day stomach flu. It was miserable. Luckily, Kendall and Art didn't catch it.

Art is doing very well. He's still working for the Mental Health Department, and he really enjoys it. He's still doing school. He should receive his certificate for drug addiction studies by the end of fall next year. He's thinking of moving on to get a degree in either psychology or sociology.

Kendall is doing wonderfully. She talks and sings a lot. Mom was doing this little quiz on a website about toddlers, and one of the questions was about a child's vocabulary at age two years. The average vocabulary for a two-year-old is about fifty words. Kendall speaks more than fifty words. She speaks about two hundred or so. She knows her ABCs and a few nursery rhymes. She repeats everything you say. She's very smart. Almost too smart sometimes.

When she knows that she's doing something she shouldn't be, she looks at me, smiles, and tries to give me a kiss so that I won't get mad at her. She's figured out how to crawl out of her crib, even though we haven't seen it yet. I walked into her room this morning and found her sitting on the floor in her room reading her books. She loves books!

Mom went on two vacations this year. She drove her motorcycle from Tahoe all the way to Milwaukee, Wisconsin. By herself, I might add. She had a great time. It was the hundredth anniversary of Harley-Davidson. She also went on a cruise for a week with some friends. She went to New Orleans, Bahamas, Cozumel, Jamaica, and the Grand Cayman.

Hope everyone has a happy holiday.

Love,
Jeanna, Arturo, and Kendall

February 20, 2004

Dear Kendall,

You started a new day care, "First Impressions." Your first day was February 11, 2004. They were having a Valentine's Day party that day as well. You came home with lots of little valentines from all the kids. The day before you started, Grandma took you over to get familiar with the place a little bit before we officially started you there. You were doing great until I left you there on your first day. You cried when I left. You cried when I picked you up. You didn't take a nap that day either. I think it was a lot for you. You have never really been with anyone other than Grandma, Bonnie, your dad, and me. This was new for you. More kids to play with. More toys and more variety than what you already had. New people. I knew that it was going to be a transition. But I didn't know it was going to be this hard.

You like going over to Grandma's house. When she comes over, you say, "Grandma's house." You go over there every morning, and then she takes you to the babysitters. You watch *Sesame Street* together every morning. You watch *The Wiggles* with Mommy every morning too. Those are your two favorite shows.

You're doing a little better now, but you still cry when Grandma drops you off. You cry when I pick you up and you say, "Go bye-bye." You're ready to go home. You're eating your meals and snacks though. You finally took a longer nap yesterday, two and a half hours. You must have been tired, and it's starting to catch up to you.

I want to ask you about your day. I usually ask you if you played with Olivia, Rachel, and Josie. These are the other girls that are close to your age. I ask you about what you had for lunch. Usually Kris (the babysitter) tells me, but I just want to hear you say it.

I think that you'll get to like the place. I like the programs and things that Kris does with the kids. Kris has talked about doing swimming lessons with the kids that are interested. You love the water, and I think it would be fun for you.

We went to Los Angeles this last weekend so that you could see your dad's side of the family. You really bonded with your Abuelita this trip. You would wake up in the morning and ask for her. You were playing with her and hugging her. It was cute. You also played with your Tia Angelica. You like both a lot more this trip. Your cousins, however, were a little too much for you. You seemed a little overwhelmed around them. I don't think you're as comfortable around them yet. You did well over all though. You did cling to me quite a bit.

You're starting to ride your bike. You can turn the pedals, but you still don't understand the turning the handlebars part yet. You peddle until you run into something and then get frustrated because you can't go where you want it to go. I think you'll be ready by summer though.

You really love your books. We read at least five books a night before bed, if not more. When you wake up in the morning, it's "read books."

You're trying to talk on the phone more now. You tend to mumble more though. You want to say so much but don't know how to quit saying it yet. It's very funny. I can usually pick out two words out of twenty. You're trying though. I'm very proud of you. I love you very much.

Love,
Mommy

April 3, 2004

Dear Kendall,

Your Abuelita, Tia Angelica, and Tio Israel came up from Los Angeles, California, last night. Today you all went to San Francisco, California, with Daddy. Mommy stayed home. You were going to see Alcatraz (the most famous prison). This will be your first time to San Francisco. I hope that you have fun.

You're talking on the phone a lot more. We know what to say to get you to talk. You've also done this thing where you say, "Hold on." You put the phone down on the bed next to you. It's too funny.

You're doing very well at the new day care. You even have a couple of friends that are close to your age: Olivia, Spencer, Sarah, Larissa (Rachael and Josie, but they aren't there anymore). You tell me that you play with the kids "eveyday." I love it when you say that word *eveyday*…color eveyday, watch TV eveyday, read books eveyday. Kris fills out a daily activity chart for me so that I know what you're doing during the day. When I pick you up, I pull that sheet out and read it out loud on the way home. I want to ask you what you learned about that day. I wait for you to reply. Sometimes you answer me, and sometimes you're not quite sure. One time, I asked you what you learned about, and you said, "Spiders." I couldn't believe that you knew what I was asking. You are so incredibly smart. I tell you to say that too. Say, "I'm smart." You say, "I mart."

You still love to read books. Now you try to read them back to us. You say a lot of the right words, but you can't say the whole thing. You try hard though. You tried to read to your Abuelita this morning, and it was very cute.

We've been teaching you to say "please" and "thank you," and you're very good at it. We went down to Carson to go shopping with Grandma, Abuelita, and Daddy. You were sitting in the back with your grandmothers, and you were playing with your Abuelita's glasses. She wanted them back. You said, "De por favor." You made her ask for them back. It was so funny. And you even said it in Spanish to her.

You can spell your name by yourself. K-E-N-D-A-L-L. You can sing the ABC song by yourself. You try to sing "Old McDonald" and some others, but it's a lot of little words for you still. We listen to your kid's CDs all the time in the car. I'm sick of hearing them. I try to tell you that it's Mommy's turn to listen to her music, but then you threw a fit if I didn't turn your CDs on. You usually end up winning. I tell Daddy, "Who wears the pants in this family?" I tell him, "It sure isn't you or myself." You're pretty demanding for a little girl.

Grandma asks you how old you are. She says, "Two." I tell you to say, "Not yet." Then you argue that back and forth a couple of times. You like to copy a lot of things. Almost everything is "I do it. I do it." You are very independent and bossy. Which is good and bad. You don't let us help you sometimes because you want to do it by yourself. You try to help with the vacuuming, sweeping, laundry, cleaning up your room, just about anything. You are very helpful.

You say please and thank you at the right time. You even say, "No, thank you."

You're affectionate. You give hugs and kisses out of the blue. Sometimes you grab my face with both hands and kiss me. It's cute. I love you.

Love,
Mommy

May 14, 2004

Dear Kendall,

We went out to eat dinner at this burger place, and you were running around as usual. I looked over, and one second you were hanging from this table, and the next second you were lying on the floor screaming. It looked as though the table hit you on the head, but it turned out that it landed on your hand. I didn't think it was broken because you were moving it. It was bruised and swollen. We let it go and just watched you for a few days.

I ended up staying home with you one day because you were sick, and we decided to take you to the doctor for your hand. Sure enough, you broke a bone in your hand. They were going to cast it and decided not to. They were surprised that you were still using it as much as you were. They thought that you were a tough little girl. We went back twelve days later for another x-ray, and there was no crack. It had healed up in less than two weeks. The doctor said, "God bless youth."

The day before Mother's Day, your kitty, Buddy, was out like usual, playing in the dirt and chasing bugs. I went out to call him, and he didn't come like he normally did. I knew something was wrong. A car hit Buddy. You were asleep at the time, but I was up all night trying to figure out how to tell you about your kitty. When I finally told you the next day, you didn't understand and said, "Bye, Buddy." I felt better after I told you, but he was the coolest cat. He was the most affectionate kitty, and you loved him a lot. He was very tolerable of you as well.

There was a Mother's Day dinner at First Impressions. The kids were supposed to make dinner for their mothers. There were picture frames handmade by the kids with their individual photos in them. You made one for me with a picture of you and a little boy named Mikey that you play with. There were also flowers for the mothers.

All the kids sang, "Happy Mother's Day" to the tune of "Happy Birthday." "Happy Mother's Day to you. Happy Mother's Day to you. Happy Mother's Day, dear Mommy, we love you too." It was very cute. You were not there though. Grandma had picked you up early, and so you didn't get to sing to me.

I stayed up with you all night the other night. You were in pain, and I kept thinking it was your two-year molars coming in because you were complaining that your teeth hurt. You woke up every hour crying. You were just so miserable. I didn't know what to do. Daddy took you to the doctor the next day. It turned out that you had a bad ear infection that was causing so much pain. We got you antibiotics and eardrops to help you get over the infection.

I think you're a tomboy. You haven't been around a lot of boys, but you sure act like one. You hurt yourself all the time. You have no fear when it comes to doing something daring. You do not know your limits. I don't know if that's a good thing or a bad thing. You were running down the hall at Grandma's house. You tripped and hit your head on her bed, giving yourself a fat bump on your forehead. You have a scratch on your shin where you ripped some skin off, and you broke your hand. Sometimes I wish you would slow down.

You are a little more affectionate now. You'll come up to me and give me hugs and kisses for no reason other than to let me know that you need some attention. I love it when you do that. I say, "Guess what?" to you, and you say, "I love you." I love being a mommy.

I love you very much.

Love,
Mom

July 9, 2004

Dear Kendall,

It's been a while. There have been a lot of changes. You are now two years old, and the terrible twos have hit. Your birthday party was fun. I made it a farm theme, and we held it at Grandma's house. The invitations were little barns with cows on the inside. I made a barn cake that took me two hours to make. I had barn animal figurines, blow-up farm animals, wind-up farm animals, farm animals to color, and handkerchiefs to wear on your heads. I read a story, "Barnyard Boogie," which is one of your favorite books. For the food, we had Kentucky Fried Chicken and sat on blankets on the grass. Grandma bought you a swing set, and all the kids were playing on it with you. Your friends that came were Zoe, Levi, Eddie, Dion, Jasmine, April, Quentin, Marcos, and his little brother.

First Impressions had a little party for you as well. They sang happy birthday to you and had a cake.

You are no longer going to First Impressions anymore. We didn't like the lack of communication between Kris and Laura. There were things going on that we were unaware of. Kris also moved her day care to another home, and you were not handling it very well. You wouldn't let your dad and I out of your sight. When we would try to put you to bed like we normally would, read books, drink your milk, and wait for you to fall asleep and then slip out, you would wake up and run for the door screaming. We are still having a hard time putting you to sleep, but I think it's getting better. I hope it's getting better.

We found out that you had been in a fight with Baby James. He's one year old. You were fighting over a pacifier, and he bit you on the arm, and you were choking him with your hands around his neck. I was really bothered by this and didn't know what to do. You had never acted like this before. You also hit Olivia, and no one mentioned anything to your dad or myself. They were trying to potty train you without asking us. You are not ready for that. Kris was going out of town and not telling us. It was just too much for you and for us. The part that bummed me out the most was the relationships that you had had with some of the children. Mikey is your favorite and Olivia. You also liked Baby James, Larissa, Sara, Cole, Benny, and Spencer. I'm going to try and coordinate playdates with Mikey so that the two of you can still play together.

You are going to a place now called Lakeshore Family Childcare. It's a young couple, Heather and Joe, around our age, who have a little boy named Giovanni and a new baby girl (born on your birthday) named Lexington. All the kids in the day care are all around two years old, and they've all been going there since they were babies. You've been there a couple of times, and we just started taking you this week. Heather said the first day you were screaming when she tried to put you down for a nap, but you eventually calmed down and fell asleep. I think you'll like it here more. The kids are all your age, and it's more structured.

They want to start you in gymnastics and take you to the beach once a week. You'll be taking field trips and swimming lessons.

The hardest part about all of this is bedtime. I just hope that you get over this soon because it's starting to frustrate your dad and me very much. I normally have a lot of patience with you, but this bedtime thing is going on, I don't. I've had to be forceful with you and spank you, and I don't like how I've been treating you. You wear my patience though.

I just want you to know that I love you very much, and I will always be there for you.

Love,
Mom

July 31, 2004

Dear Kendall,

Today was Uncle Jeff and Auntie Tina's wedding day. You did so GOOD today! You took a nap when you were supposed to. You ate dinner with everyone else. You even had salad. You really wanted cake and kept asking me for some. I kept telling you to go ask Auntie Tina. You would run over to her, but you never asked her. You listened to me when I told you to only run around in the room where we were. You opened all the wedding gifts, which was okay. They wanted you to. You didn't make a fuss once today. You went to bed when you were supposed to and by yourself. You were an absolute blessing today. Thank you! I was very proud of you. I told you that like eight times or so. I sure do love you.

You are getting better about going to bed. We used to have to wait until we fell asleep before we could slip out of the room, but now you fall asleep by yourself. We take a bath, brush your teeth, drink your milk, and read stories until your milk is gone, turn on the night-light, turn on the music, kiss you good night and sweet dreams, and walk out of the room. You don't even make a fuss. Well, most of the time, this is the new routine. It's so nice to be able to relax after putting you down, and we don't have to fight with you. Mommy and Daddy can spend a little more one-on-one time with each other.

The other day, you said the cutest thing to me. I usually ask you, "Know what?" Then I will tell you that I love you. You usually say, "I love you too." The other day though, I was in the bathroom and needed some toilet paper. You brought me up some from downstairs. You handed me the toilet paper and started to walk back downstairs. You took two steps and then turned around and asked me, "Know what?" Then you said, "I love you." It was so cute and so spontaneous. It was the sweetest thing.

Another morning, I was getting in the shower. When I walked by you in the bathroom, you said, "Mommy, you're pretty." You amaze me with some of the things that you say. You are so cute.

When I brush your hair in the morning, I tell you that your hair is very pretty and that you are a very pretty girl. You were brushing my hair for me on another day, and you said, "Mommy, you have pretty hair."

Since you've been going to Heather and Joe's house, new day care, you've been coming home with some funny things lately. You came home one day and kept asking your baby, "Do you want a time-out? Finish your lunch. Are you done?" I thought you had been in trouble at the day care. I called Heather and asked her. She said no and that it was probably her son, Giovanni, because he gets time-outs a lot.

You're doing much better in the morning now as well. The only thing is, in the morning before we leave, you say, "No go, kids." Meaning you don't want to go to day care, but when we get there, you don't cry at all. We usually drop you off and you're off playing. It's just getting you there is still a little struggle.

You play in the water a lot. You really like the water. You've been playing tea party with this little tea party set that Stacy, your Head Start teacher, brought over one morning, and you can't seem to stop playing with it. Pretty much every day, you have a tea party at some time of the day.

Since the weather has been so nice outside, you've been running through the sprinklers naked in the yard out front and at Grandma's house. You like to run through it screaming because it's cold to you. It's cute. I call you a funny naked babe.

The swings (fwings) are your favorite thing to do right now. You have a swing set at Grandma's house that you play on almost every day. You like going to any park. You're fearless though. You can swing on the big swing instead of the little baby swings. You go back and forth on them though. You also like to push the swings and watch them. You even push Mommy on the swing.

You like to watch *The Wiggles* and *Koala Brothers* in the mornings with Mom, and then you watch *Sesame Street* with Grandma at her house. Your favorite Wiggles songs are ♫ "Fruit Salad" (yummy, yummy. Step one, peel some banana. Step two, throw in some grapes. The third step, cut up some apples. Cut up some melon and put it on your plate) and "Hot Potato" (hot potato. Cold spaghetti, cold spaghetti. Mashed banana, mashed banana) ♫.

You're singing more Spanish nursery rhymes. Daddy bought some new books that he reads to you, and you've been speaking more Spanish. One of your favorite books is *Pio Peep*. You also like *Hoodwinked, Barnyard Boogie, Pajama Time, No Jumping on the Bed,* and *Biscocho.*

Picking your nose lately. You pick your nose and stick out your finger like you are offering it to someone. You ask, "Want some or quieres?" It's funny. I call you a booger face.

You can spell your name on your own. When someone asks you how old you are, you say, "Two years old."

I've been starting to have you spell more words now. I tell you to repeat after me, and we spell *cat, dog, car, ear, nose, feet, eye, ball.* I just want you to start getting the idea of how to spell some small words.

You are so precious! I love you very much.

Love,
Mom

September 4, 2004

Dear Kendall,

It's your Mommy talking about you again. You are so beautiful and amazing. You really light up my life. I love being a mom, your mom. You have been so loving lately. Today we watched our cartoons in the morning like we do every day (*Stanley, Wiggles, Jojo's Circus*), and you were lying on my lap, sitting in my lap, giving me kisses and hugs. I love it when you love me. You do it on your own, which is even better. Everyone always tells me how pretty you are, and I believe you are. It makes me feel good that people say things like that about you.

Your hair is getting so long. We still must cut your bangs at least once a month because they grow so fast. Your lips are voluptuous and full. Your eyes are almond-shaped with luscious lashes. It's no wonder why you get away with a lot of things.

I was reading to you the other night, and you covered your eyes with your hands and said, "Oh my gosh." You pulled your hands off your eyes as you were saying it. I looked at you and wondered where you got that from. You can be so dramatic.

You're favorite saying now is "What you said?" When we are talking to you and you want us to repeat it, you say, "What you said?" It's cute. You know what it means, but you say it so sweet.

I asked you if I could hug and love you. You were in a silly mood. You said, "No way, Jose."

We walked out to get into the car, and both Mommy and Daddy's cars were on. You don't like going in Daddy's car because he's the one that usually takes you to day care. I told you that we were going in Mommy's car. You said, "What a good idea."

Grandma asked you how day care was and what you did. She asked if you went to the park, played at the beach, or outside. You had to think for a minute and then said, "I don't know."

You were playing with Daddy outside driving the little remote-controlled car. You were controlling it, and Daddy asked you for a turn. You shook your finger at him and said, "No take turns, Daddy."

Pammy's niece Madigan was visiting her grandparents next door to Grandma's house, and you played with her almost every day that she was here. She is about nine years old, but you were bossing her around. You even gave her a time-out for no reason. While she was visiting though, we took you to the amusement park in town. You went on the roller coaster, the umbrella ride that goes around fast, bumper cars, the train, and the big slide. You would have kept on going if we hadn't said that it was time to stop because you needed to take a nap. You had a blast, and you didn't even get sick. We've taken you again to the amusement park since then, but none of us could go on the umbrella ride with you because we would get sick on it, and you were too little to go by yourself.

You've been really interested in watching movies lately. We usually don't let you watch very much TV, but you'll ask to watch a movie and sit through the whole movie. You really like *Monsters, Inc.*, *Toy Story*, and *Finding Nemo*. We watched *Monsters, Inc.* four times in one weekend. I think you need to cut back on your movie watching. For someone who didn't used to watch very much TV, you watch it more than you should.

We've been worried about you lately. Ever since you've been going to Heather and Joe's house (day care), you've been sick a few times, and you've had diarrhea a little more than you should. We've taken you to the doctors and were getting some tests done to see if there is something underneath that we cannot see. I don't know if it's your nerves or digestion or something else, but it's more often than it should be, so we are going to investigate further.

Your daddy and I just found out on September 2 that you are going to have a sibling. We think that you are ready for a sibling. Every time you see a baby, you want to kiss it and touch its head. You are so gentle with babies. We are so excited. Don't worry though. You will always be Mommy's baby girl, my cookie. It's referring to the book *The Difference between Babies and Cookies.* A book that talks about babies and what they do.

I love you so very much.

Love,
Mom

October 11, 2004

Dear Kendall,

The other night, you were sort of playing hide-'n-go-seek with your daddy. You would go hide in the closet where the coats are, and he would go hide. You come out running, looking everywhere for him. You would scream with excitement when you found him.

Then it was your turn to hide. Daddy went into the closet and waited for you to hide. I would help you hide, but then when he would ask where May May was. You would come out of hiding screaming and laughing. You did this every time. You would always come out of hiding. It was such a crack-up. You didn't get the idea of staying hidden.

You are totally into the movie thing now. When you are done watching one movie, you ask to watch another. You get mad at me when I tell you, "No, only one movie." You don't need to watch that much TV. I will try to get you to play with Daddy, Abuelita, or myself (she's in town right now). You don't really want to play with anyone. You're starting to play more by yourself.

Last night was fun. You and I were coloring and listening to music. You were trying hard to color in the lines. You were doing well. You seem to like blue a lot. You paint and color with it a lot.

When Daddy came home, we were dancing. Then you danced with him. It was so cute. You were dancing with your daddy. He was spinning you around, saying you were practicing for your quinceañera. You have a lot of time for practicing for that. You're only twenty-eight months old.

You went on a trip to Los Angeles again with Daddy. Daddy had to take you to the emergency room the night you got there because you had an ear infection. You kept asking for your primos. You had a good time.

We found out that your Tia Angelica was going to have a baby as well. That means that you're going to have a cousin the same age as your sibling.

Your daddy has been asked to apply for a new job at the college. We'll see what happens with that.

I love you, baby girl.

Love,
Mom

October 18, 2004

Dear Kendall,

Your Abuelita has been here for the past two weeks, and your schedule has been totally thrown off. You were going to bed around 8:30 to 9:00 p.m., but you've been staying up later than that since she's been here. I've been struggling with you to obey me and go back to your old schedule, but it doesn't seem to be working. You are fighting with me to go to bed. What used to take about a half an hour is now taking two hours or more.

Last night, you wouldn't even listen to me. I would tell you to lie down, and you would look at me and smile, like "I don't have to listen to you." I was so mad at you and frustrated. I spanked you. After a minute or two, I apologized to you and said that I loved you. I just want you to listen to me and stop disobeying. There is a reason why you need to go to bed. If you don't get enough sleep, then you'll be crabby in the morning. You laid there for about ten minutes, and then you tried to get up and play. I got mad at you again. I kept telling you that I was going to leave the room and that you could go to bed by yourself, but that didn't work either. You would start screaming until I came back into the room. You kept crying, "Mommy, Mommy, Mommy." You were breaking my heart that you would be so disobedient and make me mad instead of just going to sleep.

I used to be able to read you stories and let you fall asleep by yourself, and now I can't leave the room until you are asleep. You won't let me leave the room, and you don't go to bed by yourself anymore. I'm losing my patience with you. I hope that you get over this soon for your sake as well as mine.

Love,
Your frustrated Mom

November 1, 2004

Dear Kendall,

Last night was Halloween. Grandma, Daddy, and I took you out trick-or-treating. You wore your giraffe costume again this year. You were a hit. Everyone thought you were so cute and what a great costume you had. We took you out to the Tahoe Keys area. This is the biggest area for trick-or-treaters. There were so many kids out. You were scared at first by some of the masks that were out, but you got used to them after a while. We thought you were going to have nightmares, but you didn't.

We started on one block and just went around. We went to get in the car, and you weren't ready to go. You wanted to keep going. You were saying trick-or-treat and saying thank you to everyone that gave you candy. You started to get excited by the other kids in costumes, and it was a lot of fun so see you having a good time. You normally shy away from new people, but you were ready to knock on the next door and so on.

We say lots of pumpkins and spiderwebs. One lady had a mask on her face when she was handing out candy. You got scared and ran away crying. You did get better though. We ended up going down four streets, and you brought home half a bagful of candy.

We opened one candy for you at the first house we went to, and you held on to it almost the whole time. It ended up getting so hard from the cold that it took you forever to finish it.

You're getting better about going to bed. You will go to bed earlier now, but I still must stay in there with you for you to fall asleep, or you stay in there and play. It's still a little bit of a struggle though.

We started potty training last week. Heather (day care) said that you were interested because all the other kids were doing it and asked if we could start. You did well the first day. You went in the potty three times. Over the weekend, though, it was a little harder. I don't really know how to train to do the potty thing, so we had quite a few accidents. I was getting better with the timing, but you would sit on the potty for about five minutes, and then as soon as you would get down, you would go in the other room and pee in your pants. You really like wearing big girl panties though.

This morning, you wanted to put big girl panties on when you woke up. We tried to go potty two times before I put your clothes on. Right after I put your clothes on, I went to brush my teeth. I came back down and saw you walk into the bathroom. I followed you in there and started to take your pants off. You had started to pee in your pants, but you ended up finishing in the potty. You're trying, but I think it's a little harder when you have clothes on because you can't get your clothes off fast enough. I've caught you a couple of times sitting on the toilet on your own, but you started to pee in your clothes before you could make it. I hope that it doesn't take you long to get it, because it's a lot of work. You are getting it though. You haven't gone poop in the toilet yet. That might be a challenge since you like to poop in peace. You don't like it when someone else is in the room with you.

Love,
Mom

November 24, 2004

Dear Kendall,

You've really been into movies a lot lately. Heather and Joe were going to take the kids from day care to go see a movie, and you were not scheduled to go that day. I really wanted you to go. So last Sunday, Daddy and I took you to see *The Incredibles*. It was about superheroes trying to fit in with other people and how they saved the world. You did well. Towards the end, though, you were getting tired of sitting. You were moving from one aisle to another. You must have enjoyed it though. You saw it later on TV as a preview, and you wanted to watch it again.

We're still in the potty training stages. You do well at Heather and Joe's house, but when you're at home or with Grandma, you don't do as well. The other night, you were sitting on the couch in your panties and just peed. You didn't even try and move. You have sticker boards at both our house and Grandma's house now, and that seems to be helping a little more, but you're still having accidents. You are getting better though.

Your Grandpa Rice is coming to visit for Christmas. This will be the first time you've ever seen him. It will be interesting to know how you are with him, considering you don't really know him. It will be strange for me too. I haven't seen him in five years myself. He's so excited.

Tomorrow is Thanksgiving. This will be the first time that I've made Thanksgiving dinner. Uncle Jeff and Auntie Tina are coming over. Grandma might come over later, but she must work, and so she's making dinner at her house as well. I'll be making turkey, ham, mashed potatoes, green bean casserole, corn, and dinner rolls. We have apple and pumpkin pies, and Grandma is making the stuffing. I'm a little nervous, but I think it will be fine. Happy Thanksgiving, baby girl.

Love,
Mom

December 5, 2004

Dear friends and family,

As you can see from the photo, Kendall is growing, and she's going to be a big sister. That's right, everyone. We're having another baby. Only one more and that's it. Back to that in a minute.

Kendall is growing so fast. We are still in the process of potty training. She can make it to the potty on her own at day care, but at home and Grandma's, it's a different story. Just this morning, she was standing on our bed and just peed right there and didn't move. I was so mad.

She knows a lot of the alphabet and talks in both Spanish and English. She is so smart and so funny. She was going to work. She took my purse, came over, kissed me, and said, "I love you. I'll be back later." I asked where she was going to work at. She said, "The grocery store." I asked her what she was going to do there. She said that she was going to get chicken and fries. I was laughing so hard, and she just looked at me funny then laughed.

I asked her if she wanted some dinner the other night. I named a few things off. She said, "No, I fine." She said that Daddy had germs the other night when he went to give her a kiss. "No, Daddy, you have germs." Art didn't know what to say. He was stunned.

Art is doing well. He just started a new job this week. He was working for the county as a mental health coordinator/councilor, and now he's working for the community college working with the Spanish-speaking community to try and help them register and sign up for classes. He's going to be advising people and their options on what classes they can take.

He gives speeches to different businesses around the community. Lots of outreaching and more involved in the community. I think he'll be great at this job, but he just started, and so we'll see. The good things are that he gets paid more. He'll get a raise every year and full benefits that covers the whole family. What a blessing!

I am still working for a real estate company doing marketing. I still really like my job. They are pretty good about me being pregnant too. There's never been an employee in this company to have a baby though. So I don't know how much time I will have off when the baby comes. I'm hoping for four to five months. I just think it's too soon to be away from a baby after only two months, which is what we'd normally get in California. I'm four and a half months along and due the beginning of May.

We're supposed to find out what the sex of the baby is in January, but Art doesn't want to know. He wants it to be a surprise. I told him that we have enough surprises in our lives that knowing what the sex is will not ruin the surprise because we still don't know what the baby will look like until it's born anyway. I think it will be a boy. I'm not as sick as the last time, and I've had dreams about a little boy. I keep telling him that, but he just looks at me.

My dad is coming for Christmas this year. It will be the first time that Kendall will see her grandpa. I haven't seen him in five years as well. He's coming for about six days. This was my Christmas present from Art.

Grandma is doing well. She's working and keeping herself busy with Kendall when she gets the opportunity. No current boyfriend right now.

Happy Holidays and a Happy New Year to all!

Love,
Jeanna, Arturo, Kendall, and Baby

December 17, 2004

Dear Kendall,

Potty training. I wish you were done with the training part. You stood on our bed the other day and just peed right in the middle of our bed. You sat on the couch last night and peed on the couch. You didn't even move. When I caught you, you would put your hands over your butt and say, "No trouble" or "No spanking." I reassured you that you were not in trouble, but I was disappointed in you. You're supposed to go potty in the big girl potty, not your pants. I've told you several times that we were going to put you back in diapers if you can't go potty in the big girl potty. You usually say, "No diapers," and I tell you not to go in your pants.

You've been afraid to go poop in the potty because you hold it for so long that it usually ends up hurting you when you finally do go. I took you to the doctor and asked them if there was something else that we could do to help you out. The doctors suggested apple juice, prune juice, and more fiber. Last night, I bought you some prune juice and Dr. Pepper (soda). I mixed the two together so that it didn't taste so bad, and you ended up going in the potty all by yourself. I was so proud of you. I think you were even proud of yourself. When you were done, you got off the potty and flushed it. You said, "Bye, poopie" and waved at it. I let you have two stickers. You kept saying, "Two stickers," holding up two fingers.

Grandma takes you to the chiropractor sometimes, and the doctors' name is Harvey. The other day, I said that my back hurt. You asked if I was going to see Harvey. I took you with me yesterday. I told you that we were going to see Harvey. You asked me if I didn't feel good. I said, "No. Mommy doesn't feel good." You told me that you didn't feel good either. I asked if you needed to see Harvey too. You said, "No, I feel better."

We took you down to Horizon Casino to see Santa Claus and get your photo taken. You were afraid and didn't want to sit on his lap. There was another little girl named Jenika that we used to see at the laundromat that we saw there as well. The two of you were running down the casino, holding hands and laughing with one another like you were best friends. She had no problem sitting on Santa's lap. She went first, and when it was your turn, you didn't want to go. But then Jenika sat on his lap with you, and you were fine. We got your picture taken with the both of you. It was cute.

To try and get our attention when we're doing something, you say, "Pst-a." "Hey, pst-a." You are just so funny. I love you very much.

Love,
Mom

December 28, 2004

Dear Kendall,

This was a very nice Christmas. Probably the best Christmas that I can remember. Your Grandpa Rice came to visit us for six days. The first day, you were hesitant towards him because you didn't really know him, but the next day, you wanted him to play with you. Grandma came over to see us, and you didn't want to share his time with anyone. You wanted Grandma to stop getting involved, and you wanted Grandpa to go upstairs with you in your room so that you could play with him by yourself.

We had Christmas at our house. Grandma and Uncle Jeff do not really get along, but for Christmas, they made things work between the two of them. The family that was here: Grandma, Grandpa, Uncle Jeff, Auntie Tina, Bobby, Travis, Daddy, you, and Mommy. We had dinner and then opened gifts from each other. Everyone got along and had a good time. It was so amazing to see the togetherness of everyone. I think you and I both had a lot to do with it. You, because everyone loves you and adores you, and myself because I always try to make things work out between our family. This holiday meant so much to me.

Uncle Jeff made a CD for everyone to take home with them of all the pictures that he took with his camera. Of course, 90 percent of the CD is of you.

The whole time he was here, you would ask where Grandpa was and want to go see him. You would go downstairs and want him to play with you. I couldn't believe how fast you bonded with him. It was so nice to see you and my dad together. It was the first time he had ever seen you in person, so it was nice for him as well. He went back to Oklahoma today. You asked where Grandpa was when you woke up, and I told you that he went home on an airplane.

You also left this morning to go see your other family in Los Angeles with Daddy. The two of you drove down there. You went to see your Abuelita, Tia Angelica, Tio Israel, and all your cousins. You got excited when we asked you if you wanted to go see your Abuelita. It's almost like having Christmas all over again.

I hope you had a very happy holiday with all your family. I love you so very much!

Love,
Mom

January 3, 2005

Dear Kendall,

Your daddy decided to take you to Las Vegas spur of the moment while you were in Los Angeles. He didn't tell me that you were going until you were already back. I was beginning to worry. I felt that it was not a good idea to take you to a busy city during a big holiday, especially New Year's week. It was so busy and crowded. I was not happy about that.

You had a lot of fun with your cousins down in Los Angeles. You played mostly with Marcopolito, Chelita, Aaron, and Andres. It took just a little bit to warm up because you hadn't seen them since the last time you were down there, but once you warmed up, you didn't want them to leave. Daddy even asked you if you wanted to go home with them. You got in the car and everything, but when it was time to pull away, you wanted Daddy to come, and you cried. You did go in the car with them the next day, only because you knew that Daddy was going in another car to the same place.

You played with your Abuelita and your Tia Angelica as well. You got some new toys and babies from them.

When it was time to come home, you didn't want to. Daddy was telling you that it was time to go home and see Mommy. You said that you didn't want to go home and see Mommy.

It was snowing hard after you both drove down to Los Angeles. We received so much snow in such a short period that the roads were closed off and on for three days. I was beginning to wonder if you were going to get home and when. It was supposed to snow all next week as well. You and Daddy started to make your way home on New Year's Day, but the fog was so thick that you had to stay in another town overnight until it passed. You finally made it home yesterday afternoon. I was so happy to see you both. I cried and worried for days. I'm just glad that you both made it home safely.

Now you're not feeling well though. You had a fever of 103.5°F. You also have a rash on your bottom. You're not really eating. You've gotten sick a couple of times, and you have diarrhea. I'm going to have your Grandma take you to the doctor tomorrow. I can tell that you don't feel well because all you want to do is lie on the couch and have someone hold you. It's nice that you're mellow, but I know that it's not fun to be sick. I hope you feel better soon.

Love,
Mom

January 10, 2005

Dear Kendall,

Well, we went to the doctor for Mommy on January 7. I had an ultrasound of your new sibling. The nurse thinks that it's going to be a girl, but I still think she's wrong. I saw the pictures as well, and it looked like a boy to me. They weren't sure anyway. I guess we won't find out until the baby is born now.

I wanted you to go and be a part of the baby as much as you can, but you didn't care. It didn't really look like a baby to you. All you could really see was the outline and some movement, perhaps some bones and organs, but nothing that would really resemble a baby to you.

That night, the baby was moving in my stomach, and Daddy and I were trying to get you to touch my stomach to feel it move, but you didn't want to. I don't think you really know what's going on.

Ever since you got back from Los Angeles, you've been going to bed earlier, which has been nice. I don't know if it's because you've been sick, but you've been going to sleep a lot easier and faster instead of playing around for over an hour. I can get some time to relax to myself now. I really like this newer routine.

When you came back sick, I decided to call you another nickname, "bug." I call you bug or buggy now. I think it sort of fits your personality as well. You can be a bug sometimes. So now when I ask you what your name is, I ask you, "Is your name Kendall, Boober, May May, or Bug?" Depending on your mood, you'll pick one of them and tell me. I also ask if you're my cookie. Cookies are sweet, so I call you my cookie.

Potty training is getting better as well. You still have some accidents here and there, but lately, you've been going to the bathroom by yourself. You'll walk into the bathroom by yourself and go potty. The only thing is, you don't really wipe. You do better when we're out in public than at home though. You usually let me know when you must go to the bathroom, and we go. The other day, we went to McDonald's, and you were playing in the play area. You stopped what you were doing and said that you had to go potty. You told me to stay where I was and that you could do it by yourself. I followed you anyway. You pretty much did it all by yourself, except washing your hands. I had to help you out with that. I'm so proud of you. You are doing well. It's just taking time.

The other day, you were playing with your babies. I asked you where you were going. You said that you were going to the store to see Huckleberry Pie and get some peanuts. I was laughing because it was so unexpected.

Your new thing lately is also your better dramatization of how you talk. You put your hands up and out and say, "I don't believe it." You emphasize the "believe it" part when you say it. It's cute.

We took you to McDonald's to play last night. There was this little boy, just under a year and a half, trying to climb up the stairs. You were watching him from the top. As he decided to climb back down, you followed him. You patted him on the head a couple of times. As soon as he got down to his dad, you ran back up the stairs to go down the slide. It was almost like you were watching over him to make sure he was going to get down okay.

I think you'll be a great big sister. I love you!

Love,
Mom

February 11, 2005

Dear Kendall,

You've started helping me a lot more. When it's time to clean up or put things away, you've been helping me more. I must tell you sometimes, though, when you don't want to help that I'll put your toys in time-out. You won't stay in time-out, but you don't like it when I put your toys in time-out. It seems to work most of the time. The other day, though, I said that I was going to put your bowling pins in time-out, and you said, "Okay."

When we have trouble getting you to eat, we say that Pete will eat it if you don't. Most of the time, you say no and eat, but the other day, I said, "Are you sure you don't want any more?" You said, "Call Pete. He'll eat it." You're getting too smart for your own good.

You've surprised us yet again with the things that you say. Grandma called me the other day to tell me something you said. She said that you were lying on the floor with your baby, and you turned to her to say, "I'm feeling bored."

You and I were at Grandma's house and waiting for her to come home from work, and you were playing with this little basketball hoop on the window. I asked you where the basketball was if it was in your toy box. You said, "Maybe so. Go look for it." I didn't know what to say but laugh.

Lately, in the morning, Daddy will try and help get you ready so that I'm not late in the morning, and you won't let him. You tell him that he has germs, and you fight with him when he tries to help you with your clothes or shoes. You've been really mean to him lately. I'm sure that it hurts Daddy's feelings, but he still tries. You usually yell for me and start crying. I've been telling you that you're being mean to Daddy and that he's just trying to help. I don't know how much of that you understand though.

When we take you to school now, you say, "No kids." I tell you OK. Then you usually ask Grandma "Pick me up early." You don't fight us in the morning anymore, but you try to come up with something for not going. Once you get there, you're fine. You act like we aren't even there now. A lot of the time, you don't want to leave there when we come to pick you up.

One day, you asked if Grandma could pick you up early. I told you that I would ask her. You said, "You ask." I ended up having to pick you up instead. I walked in, and you said, "No. Grandma pick me up early." It was after five, and so it was already past early, but you wanted Grandma to pick you up instead of me.

Heather and Joe got a new puppy for Giovanni. They named him Gazzy. The other day, you saw a dog that looked like him. You said, "That looks like my doggy." I asked you what your doggy's name was. Then you said, "Gazzy." I asked if Giovanni knew this. It was cute. I guess all the kids at school consider Gazzy their puppy as well.

You were doing good at school about going to the bathroom on your own, but lately, you've been peeing in your pants at nap time, which you didn't do before. You are doing better about going poop in the potty though. You still have occasional accidents in your pants, but mostly pee. Some days you'll just stand there and pee, not even trying to move. I'm not sure why you do it though. We keep telling you that big girls wear big girl panties and that you need to go in the big girl potty if you need to go potty, not in your pants, or we'll have to put diapers back on you.

You've been pretty good about going to bed as well. I've stopped giving you juice for bed. The only thing we give you now is water. You don't really like it, but if you want something to drink, you'll drink it. We still put a diaper on at nap time and at night because you pee a lot at night. You ask if we can put big girl panties on top, but I tell you that if you wear big girl panties, you can't have water. You usually say, "No, water," meaning that you would rather have water, so I give you a choice.

The past few days, I haven't been feeling well. I told you that it's time for bed and that Mommy's going to bed. I fall asleep before you, but when I come to check on you an hour or so later, you were asleep under your covers. You've been getting better about going to sleep by yourself. I'm trying to break you of the habit of falling asleep with Mommy or Daddy, especially before the baby comes because we won't be able to do that every night.

I've been trying to coordinate more playdates for you. One because I'm tired and I'm having a hard time trying to keep you entertained and because it's nice for both of us to visit other people our own age.

We went to McDonald's the other night, and you played with Jenny's two kids, Kieran and Jacob. You had fun and didn't want to go. We've had Jasmine and April over to stay the night a couple of times. You love Jasmine. They came over last week, and you followed Jasmine around like a little puppy. You copied everything that she did and wanted to play everything that they did. We've also had Zoe and Levi, our neighbors, over to play a few times. You just have so much fun when there are other kids to play with. It's good for you, and I get a break.

I think that you'll be a great big sister. I love you!

Love,
Mom

March 1, 2005

Dear Kendall,

I've been trying to keep you busy and have a social life with other kids because it's getting harder for me to keep up with you now because of the pregnancy. The other day, we had Kieran and Jacob over with their puppy, Bunny. You really liked Bunny. She's a pug and small. She was licking your face, and you were having so much fun. While they were over, you were all upstairs in your room playing. Kieran came down to tell us that you had taken your pants off and peed on the floor. Then that night, we went to see Autumn's kids, Josh and Andrew. You were having so much fun that you didn't want to leave.

Andrew is a baby, five months old. I was holding him in my lap, and you didn't get jealous at all. In fact, you came over and asked if you could hold him. You sat down next to me and held him for a short period. It kind of surprised me because you were so good with him.

The other night, I was putting you to bed and left the room. I came back a few minutes later to check on you, and you were in the crib. I told you that if you wanted to stay there, you could, and you did. You slept there all night. I don't know if it's because of the baby coming or if you just want to be different. You are different from most kids your age. You are very smart!

Madigan is in town this week, and you've been playing with her as well. We were on our way out to Bonnie's to see Jasmine, April, and Maddie a couple of nights ago. We were driving, and I told you that we were going out to see the girls. You said, "That is good logic." I didn't know what to say. I've never heard you use that word before and use it in the right context.

Kieran started going to day care this week. Jenny is taking him to Heather and Joe's. I guess he was telling Joe that he was at your house, and you took your pants off and peed on the floor. Joe and Jenny were laughing because he was telling you. They said that he did well. Jenny kept saying that he was going to go to the same school as you. He kept saying that he was going to Kendall's house. I think you two will have fun when you go to school on Wednesday. I love you!

Love,
Mom

March 19, 2005

Dear Kendall,

I've been working the last four Saturdays to make up time I took off from work for when I hurt my ankle. These last three Saturdays have been known as "Boober/Daddy days." He's been taking you out and playing with you. The first weekend, you went bowling, swimming, and played in the snow. The second Saturday, you went to a children's museum in Carson City. They had different learning areas set up where you could go shopping, play doctor, and read books. You didn't want to leave there. This last Saturday, Daddy took you over to this place called Kids Zone, but it was closed. You ended up going to the park and lunch instead. Today it's raining outside, and so you're going to help Daddy with the laundry.

I think it's been very good for the both of you to spend time together. You've grown closer to Daddy, and he's getting to know you a little more as well. You've even been speaking a little Spanish. You really enjoy his time because it's just the two of you, so he gives you all the attention. Daddy normally wears a hat, and so we bought you a hat for your special days with Daddy.

We took you to the Child Development Center at the local community college yesterday. You are going to start going to preschool next month. We took you over to visit and show you where you were going to start going to school. You walked in, and there was so much to do. You played on the slide, made a paper flower picture, and played outside with the kids in the sandbox. You didn't want to leave. You had fun. We think that you will get a lot out of this. You will learn more and be more challenged. It might be a little overwhelming at first because there are a lot more kids than you're used to. There are about twenty-five kids in the class. There are no babies in the class either. We're going to take you a few times before we officially take you. You will be going three days a week: Monday, Thursday, and Friday all day. The rest of the week, you will be going to Grandma's house.

The school director said that you should be fine at first, but then reality will kick in, and you might have a breakdown, and so we would expect it. I think you'll do fine because there is so much to do. Lots of art projects, which are what you like too.

A few things you've said lately. You were lying on the floor at Grandma's house, and you heard the phone ring. You sat up and said, "I think someone's trying to call me." You went to pick up your play cell phone and started talking.

You came up to me one morning and said, "Do you know where my wallet is?" You said a full sentence that I was not expecting, and it threw me off. I told you where I thought it was, and you found it.

You brought me your stuffed flower and said, "Here you go, Mommy. For extra beauty." I almost cried.

Daddy and I were talking the other day about Daddy going to the doctor to get a checkup. You were listening and said, "Daddy doesn't have a baby." Referring to Mommy being pregnant, and Daddy wasn't.

You played with Autumn's kids the other day—Jacob, Joshie, and Andrew. I told you how proud of you Mommy was because you played very nicely with the kids. I said that you had lots of friends. You said, "Yeah, boyfriends."

I try to always tell you when I'm proud of you. The other day, you said, "You're proud of me. I went potty in the big girl potty and not in my pants. I was a good girl."

I would have to say that 85 to 90 percent of the time, you are a very good girl, and I am very proud of you. There was one night, though, that just blew me away. It was at the beginning of this month. Daddy was at work. Grandma was at home sleeping and you, and I were at home. The night started off with you not listening to anything I said. You spit food at me. You were very defiant. Then I tried to put you in your room, and you were screaming. I would close your door and tell you to stay in your room. You would come out and scream at me. I then tried to change your poopie diaper, and you kicked me in the stomach three times. You didn't even want to go to bed. I had to fight with you about that as well. I spanked you about twenty times that night, and it didn't seem to faze you. I was getting so frustrated.

Daddy finally came home from work, and I was crying because I didn't know what else to do. I ended up going to bed, and Daddy sat you down and talked to you. He told you that you were very mean to Mommy and that he was not happy with you. He ended up reading to you and putting you to bed. That was the worst night ever as far as being a mother.

The next day, I sat you down and told you how much you hurt Mommy and that Mommy was very disappointed in you. I said that I loved you, but you were very mean to Mommy. I made you say sorry to me. You were like a completely different child the next day. It hasn't happened since, and I hope it never does again.

I love you very much.

Love,
Mom

April 4, 2005

Dear Kendall,

Today was your first full day of preschool. We started taking you last week. Grandma took you two days, I took you one day, and Daddy took you one day. The day I took you, you said that you liked your new school and didn't want to leave. You seemed like you were doing well, until today. You had a hard time. I was nervous about taking you and just dropping you off, so I had Grandma go with you and stay for a while. I went as well, but I didn't stay. You didn't want Grandma to leave. Grandma came back around nap time to see how you were doing. She just watched you for a while. Daddy came to see how you were doing as well. You ended up not taking a nap. The teachers ended up giving you a book to read by yourself quietly. Overall, you had a pretty good day. You moped a lot, but you played and had lunch as well. You didn't have one accident in your pants either. I am very proud of you. You did a lot better than I thought.

I, on the other hand, cried all the way to work after I left your school. I can't believe how fast you're growing, and I get nervous when you start something new. This was a big day for both of us.

You will be going to school three days a week: Monday, Thursday, and Friday. All day long. Grandma picked you up a little early today, and when she got there, you were outside drawing on the ground with chalk.

Last weekend, Daddy and I took you to the Kids Zone Museum. It's a place where they have different areas set up for you to play and learn. You played with the babies a lot. You also played in the kitchen area. You made the babies some food to eat. You played in the jungle gym area and jumped on mats. All three of us ended up doing art projects too. You mainly played in the paint on paper. You had a great time.

Then we went to Chuck E. Cheese's Pizza for dinner. You got scared when the Chuck E. Cheese character came out to sing though. It was a fun but long day.

You had a cold for a few days with a fever. Grandma took you to the doctor to have you checked out to make sure you were fine. The doctor looked in your ears and told you that you had penguins in one ear and caterpillars that turned into butterflies in the other. You remembered what he said and told me about it when I came to pick you up later.

You were at Grandma's house eating graham cracker snacks. They were Dora snacks. On the back was a backpack. You told Grandma that it was a *mochilla*. Grandma asked you what that meant. You said, "It means backpack in Spanish, Grandma." You taught Grandma a new Spanish word.

The other night, you didn't want Daddy to read you books before bedtime. You looked at me and started to cry and said, "I love you, Mommy." It was so cute. It made me get all teary-eyed. I love you so much.

Love,
Mom

April 28, 2005

Dear Kendall,

Well, you are doing very well with school. Better than I thought you were going to do. You were a little intimidated by all the kids because you went from about six to eight kids to about twenty-five. You're learning a lot of new things and making new friends. You've made projects about nursery rhymes. "Jack Be Nimble," you made a candlestick. "Humpty Dumpty," you took a picture with Humpty on a brick wall. "Hickory Dickory Dock," you made a mouse on a clock. "Little Miss Muffet," you made a spider. Then you've learned about numbers and counting, spiders, worms, caterpillars, butterflies, ladybugs, dragonflies, beetles, and ants. You've gone to the gym at the college a couple of times, and you enjoy that. They take out bouncy balls and let you all run free in the gym.

The hard part for you and school is when Mommy and Daddy leave in the morning. You start to cry a little, but then one of the teachers takes you, and then you're fine. You don't really take naps at school like you should either. So you've been coming home and going to bed earlier than normal. Perhaps because it's still all new to you. Overall, you've enjoyed going to school.

The other day, you were at Grandma's house taking a bath, and you kept saying, "Como esta."

You were playing with Grandma at her house, and you were making each other laugh. You stopped and said, "I'm just cracking me up."

The other day, both Daddy and I took you to school. I was leaving, and Daddy was staying with you for a little bit. You did have an ear infection that you were still getting over. I left, and you were crying. Daddy thought that it was your ears that were hurting you, and so he decided to take you to Grandma's house instead of leaving you at school. I called Grandma's house to see how you were doing, and she said that you were fine and running around. Grandma asked you why you were crying this morning. Did your ears hurt? You said, "No, I was sad because I missed Mommy." I told her to take you back to school.

The more we've taken you to school, the less you've cried. The other day, I asked if you cried when I left. You said, "I cried just a little." You held your thumb and first finger up to show me how little.

You were playing with your Barbies at Grandma's house and told Barbie to just sit down and think about it. I guess she was in trouble or something.

When Mommy was little, about four or five years old, Grandma had tried to put me in a commercial. I was supposed to say, "This milk tastes so good, Ms. Kitty." Instead, I said, "This milk tastes good, Ms. Kitty" softly. Grandma was telling this story to someone yesterday, and when we got home, you were trying to tell it. "This milk so good, Ms. Kitty." You kept repeating it for about an hour. It was so funny how you just picked it up so fast and then thought it was so funny that you just kept saying it and laughing.

We've been trying to prepare you for becoming a big sister soon. We still don't know what gender the baby is, but we talk to you about the baby a lot. You've felt the baby move in Mommy's tummy a few times. I don't think you really understand it all yet, but I think you have an idea. We wanted to get a gift for you from the baby so that it would help the transitioning. We got you a book *I'm a Big Sister* and a Barbie scooter. We're going to give it to you when you come to meet the new baby at the hospital. We will be having the baby in four days. I hope that you enjoy your new baby.

I'm starting to get nervous about the new baby coming. I think I'm more nervous about the responsibility that comes with the new baby as well as how you are going to handle having another sibling in the house full time. Like I said before, I think you'll be a great big sister. I just think it will be tough at first.

I want you to know, though, that even with a new baby coming into our lives, I will still love you very much. I have so much love for you that I just hope I have room for loving another baby. You are Mommy's little princess.

Love,
Mommy

May 17, 2005

Dear Kendall,

It's official now. You are a big sister. You are a very good big sister as well. Your sister was born on May 2, 2005. You came every day to the hospital to see Kasandra and me. You always want to see her, hug her, and kiss her. You always want to hold her too, but not for very long. You soon say that she's too heavy for you. You are a great helper to her too. You have made it your job to oversee her Binky when she cries. You must give her the Binky. Sometimes you're almost too helpful though. Even when she makes a noise, you want to give her the Binky.

Before your sister was born, I had to go to the hospital to take some tests. I told you that I was going to the hospital, and you wanted to go with me to get the baby.

Your sister gave you a scooter when you came to see her in the hospital. You were so excited that you wanted to go out and ride the scooter immediately. I thought that might be a good present. What a nice sister you have.

You were reading to your baby dolls the other night and telling them that they were good babies and that you were so proud of them. "I'm so proud of you, baby."

You are really starting to like school. Each day, you come home with some type of project that you made. You're starting to come out of your shell and making the other kids laugh all the time. You're even starting to take naps more often. You're even giving kids at school nicknames. I picked you up the other day and said hi to Molly. You said that her name was Stinky Molly. I asked why that was her name, and you told me because she tooted.

You had your first performance at the college the other day for Multicultural Day. Your class was the first ones to perform. Your class danced to two songs. You were dressed up as a little Indian girl with two braids in your hair. It was so cute. You were shaking your arms and butt. I was filming you on the camera, and I started to cry. They were happy tears. I was so proud of you.

You're learning a lot in your class. This month, you are learning about the oceans, able to recognize what's in the ocean as far as animals and shells, and dance and listen to music. You try science experiments to see what kinds of things float or sink. You counted and sorted fish by color. You painted and did little crafts. You read stories with your class about the ocean and things in the ocean. You played in the pool and pretended to dive in. And my favorite was the little doll that you made of yourself with the one strand of long hair at the beach.

We went to the beach the other day. It was Mommy, Daddy, Grandma, Kasandra, and yourself. You looked so cute in your bathing suit. You built sandcastles with Grandma and chased Daddy and Grandma around with water, trying to get everyone wet. You love the water.

You've started a new thing lately with "watcha me" or "watcha this."

I love you very much.

Love,
Mom

June 24, 2005

Dear Kendall,

You are growing up some much. You always want to do everything on your own. You are so independent. You can do a lot of things by yourself, which is nice, but I like the fact that you still need me for a few things.

You turned three years old this month. We took you down to get birthday stuff for your birthday, and you picked out Elmo. It was Elmo themed, and we held it at the Parks and Recreation Center. We had a barbecue, hamburgers, and hot dogs. Since it was at the park, all the kids were able to play at the park. A couple of your friends from school came. Logan and Dru Chapman and Allon. The other people that came were Grandma, Abuelita, Bonnie, Jasmine, April, Autumn, Jacob, Joshie, Andrew, America, Gabriela, Colleen, Cole and Conner, Tom, Gabriela, Gaby, and Kristi. You got lots of presents. The cake was Sesame Street with Big Bird and Elmo on it. After the party was over, we went to see Heather and Joe because it was Lexington's birthday as well. She was turning one year old.

We have our first parent/teacher conference next week at your school. That sounds so weird to say. You are warming up a little more at school. You still don't say very much to your teachers, but you are making lots of friends. You play with Kelsey Jean, Allon, and Anna the most. You also play with Jack, Molly, Logan Chapman, Annabella, Emarie, and Avery. You have a lot of friends and like to make them laugh.

This month in class, you are learning about farm animals and farming. You're dressing up in farm clothes—overalls, plaid and flannel shirts, farm dresses, aprons, and cowboy hats. You ride on horses and dress up in farm animal costumes. You are doing art projects with corn and hay and eating corn on the cob and popping corn.

Grandma just moved last week into a new place. It's located on two dead-end streets, so there is very little traffic. While we were moving things around, you were outside playing on your bikes and in the dirt by yourself all day long for three days. You had a lot of fun. I think you'll like her new house. You even have your own room over there now.

You are still doing well with Kasandra. You really bond with her very well. She's fond of you as well. She tries to follow your voice a lot. The hardest part is at night when I'm trying to put you down for bed and Kasandra wants to eat. All you want to do is love her and pay attention to her instead of going to bed. So far, this is the hardest thing about having two kids.

You always want to touch her and love her when you come home from school. She's going to start school in the infant room at your school starting July. When we walk into the school, you point to her room and say, "That's sissy's school."

I love you very much.

Love,
Mom

July 27, 2005

Dear friends and family,

A lot has happened lately, and I'm sure that you're all wondering how the new baby is. Let me get you all up to speed.

Kendall turned three years old in June. Threes are a nightmare! She can be so wonderful and wants to do things on her own, become more independent and help, but now is when they are learning to talk back and be more defiant. The times when you tell them, "No, don't touch that," and they look at you and touch it just to see what your reaction will be. Oh, I don't like this stage of the game. I've heard of the terrible twos, the horrible threes, and I heard that fours are worse. I thought that kids were supposed to be a blessing. They sure don't feel like little blessings sometimes. And then there are times when they do something bad and then look at you and say, "I love you, Mommy." Did I say that I love being a mom? Boy, what a challenge. I think this is why mothers work instead of being stay-at-home moms, so they don't go nuts.

So now that I vented a little…Kendall is three years old. She started preschool in April. She really likes her school. She's always doing some sort of craft and learning something. They sing this song at school about the planets, presidents, and oceans, so I know that she's slowly learning that much. No, really, she's learning a lot. They celebrated her birthday at school. I made cupcake ice cream cones. I brought them as a project for the kids to decorate them on their own. They made her stand on a chair in front of the class, and they sang to her.

She had her first presentation at school as well. They sang two songs and danced to them. They were shaking their buns to "La Bamba." I cried when I was recording it. My little girl is growing up. She's starting to speak more Spanish now as well. The other day, she was playing with her dolls and told them, "No puede ser, no comida." (It can't be, no food.) She understands a lot of Spanish but replies mostly in English.

Kendall does well with Kasandra as well. She loves her baby sister. The other day, Kasandra was crying, and I couldn't get her to stop. I tried changing her, feeding her, holding her, and nothing was working. Kendall went over to her, put a blanket on her, put her pacifier in her mouth, and she fell asleep. She tries to read her stories and wants to play with her. Kendall oversees the pacifier when she cries. Sometimes I think she does better with her than I do. She always asks for her and loves her. She's very picky about who touches her baby. Kasandra is in the same school as Kendall, different room, and doesn't want to leave her in her classroom without her.

Since I've been going back to work, Kasandra's been going to the same school as Kendall. It's three different areas—infants, toddlers, and preschool. We were having some trouble with her taking a bottle at first, but she's getting better. She's already two months old, and it seems like she's always been around. She's already smiling and laughing. She always watches Kendall and follows her with her eyes.

The hardest part about having two is bedtime. Kasandra always wants to eat at the same time Kendall is going to bed. I feel bad when I must tell Kendall no because I have to go feed her sister. Kendall has been rejected a little, but it's slowly getting better. Especially since everything is still new and getting adjusted. They're pretty much on the same schedule though, which is good.

Art is doing well. He's making a name for himself in Tahoe. He's working at the community college and trying to recruit people to take more English classes. He's also in a Lake Tahoe leadership group that tries to make things happen for our community. He's trying to create a program in Tahoe for young children to be able to go and do indoor activities. A place where the kids can go after school or during the wintertime to play. He's very well-known in Tahoe now. I've lived here my whole life, and people know him better than me. He's also taking classes online to get a degree in social science. He's doing very well.

I am officially back to work now. I'm working part-time for a couple of weeks, and then I'll be going back full time. I'm still not fully adjusted to going back to work. The first day Kasandra went to school, I made it about four hours before I had a breakdown and started crying because I missed her. I'm getting better, but I'm just going to start out part-time. I'm still doing graphic design for a real estate company.

We are one big happy family now. No more coming in the future either. We are done. I had my tubes tied when I had Kasandra. I told Art if he wanted any more children, he would have to wait until he got married to his second wife. We're happy with what we have for now. I'll keep you all informed of all our lives at Christmas.

Love,
Jeanna, Arturo, Kendall, and Kasandra

August 25, 2005

Dear Kendall,

You don't seem like a little girl to me anymore, unless you're having a tantrum because you don't get your way, that is. You're starting to look like a young lady. My little girl is growing up so fast.

You had another performance at school the other day. They had a graduation performance for the kids that were moving on from preschool to kindergarten. There were six graduates. Your class did a couple little dances and songs (Zig Zag dance, "Baby Beluga," "I'm Something Special"), and then there was a slide show of all the kids in your school, including the infant room where your sister is. Every time you saw a picture of Kasi, you would say out loud, "That's my sister." It was very cute.

You did very well too. You got into it and knew all the moves to the dances and even knew the words to the songs. Every now and then, you'll sing parts of them at home.

You really like to dance. I want to put you in some sort of activity. I just can't decide what to put you in—dance, soccer, or gymnastics. You really like all of them.

Grandma's been taking you to swim lessons at the local pool. You've been taking lessons for almost a month now. Before you started taking classes though, Daddy and I took you to the pool to play around in the water. You wanted to jump off the side of the pool, go down the slide, and jump off the diving board in the deep end. You really are a daredevil. It appears you have very little fear. Which is good and bad. I'm afraid that one of these times, you're going to hurt yourself.

More funny things out of your mouth...

You were over at Grandma's house. She asked you if you were hungry and what you wanted to eat. You said, "Sausage and eggies." You eat that a lot at Grandma's. Then you paused and said, "Actually, I want a Pop-Tart."

When she was changing out of her work clothes, you said, "Grandma, I don't want to see your bootie."

You went for a bike ride with Grandma and Kasi over by her house. You went down this steep hill and almost hurt yourself. You were going too fast and almost lost control of your bike. It scared you, and you fell on the grass near the bottom and fell off. I think it scared you and Grandma more than anything. You went for another bike ride later, and when you got close to the hill again, you said, "The hill scared the crap out of me."

You and Grandma were playing like you were fighting. You put your hands up next to your face, making fists. In a deep voice, you asked Grandma if she wanted a knuckle sandwich.

Playing with Daddy at home, and he was trying to tell you to do something. You didn't want to listen to him. You wanted him to listen to you. You told him, "Listen to my words."

Daddy talks in Spanish a lot, thinking that you won't understand him sometimes. He said something the other day, and you picked up on it. You were playing with your dolls and said, "Come caca." Art was shocked and said that if his mom heard you, he would be in big trouble. It means, "Eat poop."

Lately, you've been doing something—watching TV, playing with your toys or just outside, and you'll run up to me and tell me that you love me. It's very cute. A couple of times, you've told me that you love me while crying or whining. I tell you that you don't have to cry about it.

You absolutely adore your sister. You always want to touch her and love her. You've even picked her up a few times and tried to carry her. We're trying to teach you not to do that because we're afraid that you're going to drop her one of these times.

When we come home from school, you ask if you can touch her. I tell you that you must wash your hands first. There's been a few colds going around in your room, and I don't want your sister to get sick.

We went to get bagels from the Bagel Bakery one day. Grandma, you, and I went in the car. Daddy walked with Kasi over. You cried the whole way there, two blocks, because you were afraid that Daddy was going to take your baby. You didn't want Daddy to take your baby. You wanted her to come with us instead. It was very sweet. You are very protective when we take her to your class. You make sure to let all the kids know that she is your baby sister.

You and Kasi were in the car, and we were going to a friend's house. You were in the back laughing, and she would, in return, laugh back at you. You were both laughing at each other, and it was so cute. She tries to copy you, and you both just enjoy one another. I hope that lasts down the road.

You were lying on the couch with her, and you told me to take your picture. You were both wearing princess crowns on your heads. I said, "Look at my two princesses." I love you both very much. You are my girls.

You went with Daddy to Los Angeles this weekend. You went to Chela's house most of the time you were there. You went swimming in the pool at their house and played with all your cousins. You played with Chelita the most. She told Daddy that she felt like you were her sister. She really enjoyed playing with you. There is only one other of your cousins that's around your age, and that's Evelyn. You played with her too, but she's a little rougher because she has older brothers.

You, of course, played a lot with your Abuelita. The other night at the park, you were whining about wanting to call your Abuelita to come over and play with you. You didn't understand that she lived out of the area and couldn't just come over with a quick phone call. It was very cute. You were really excited about going to see your Abuelita when Daddy told you that you were going to Los Angeles to see her.

You were able to see Diego. This is Tia Angelica and Tio Israel's new baby. Daddy said that you were being very protective of him as well. You are so good with babies. I love you, sweetheart.

Love,
Mom

October 29, 2005

Dear Kendall,

It's almost Halloween again. You are going to be a giraffe for the third year in a row. It's hard for you to wear the hood over your head without the costume going up your butt. You are a little taller than last year. Kasi is going to wear the costume you wore when you were her age, the little dragon. It looks just as cute on her as it did you. You look very similar in it. I was comparing your photos in the same costume, and you look like one another. You both have the same eye shape, nose, and lips.

You think you are such a big girl. You try to carry Kasi now. You've moved her a few times from one direction to another when I've been out of the room. You hold her on your lap and then stand her up. You make me nervous sometimes. I walked into the living room a couple days ago from the kitchen, only to find Kasi face down on the floor still attached to her bouncy chair. You had turned her over. You didn't hurt her, but I heard her making a moaning sound. I asked you what you were doing and turned her over. It scared me.

You do love your sister though. You told her the other day, "I love you so very much." She loves you as well. Every time she sees you, she smiles. You make her laugh all the time.

You were at Grandma's the other day and said, "I have no unfinished business." I believe you were playing with your dolls when you said it. We are unsure where you heard that.

Grandma and I took you to a company, John Robert Powers, presentation. This woman took one look at you and said that she would love to put you in movies and commercials. She said that you are very beautiful. John Robert Powers is a private school for acting, singing, dancing, and modeling. I really wanted to put you in the school, but the school and training is in Reno, Nevada, and we would have to drive down once a week. It would be a lot of work, and it was too much money for us right now. It starts at $3,000 for forty weeks. Daddy and I decided not to do it. We wanted you to enjoy being a kid and not feel pressured into being a model or something. We felt that you would be better in a sport up here instead. If it happens down the road, great.

You are very shy and take a long time warming up to people that you are not familiar with. There is a girl named Ashley that works with Daddy whom you've met a few times when we've gone to see him at work. You were sick with a viral infection and didn't want to send you to school. Grandma was working and couldn't watch you. Daddy and I both couldn't really take the day off, and so Ashley offered to take you for the day. We asked you if you wanted to go to her house without Mom and Dad, and you said you were okay with it. Sure enough, Daddy took you over there and stayed with you for about fifteen minutes, and then he told you he was leaving. You didn't cry or anything. You did better than we all thought. I called in the middle of the day, and you were watching a movie and having a snack. Ashley said that you were doing very well. She said that you needed some time to warm up before you started talking to her, but that you did great otherwise. Even when I came to pick you up, you wanted to show me the swings and walked back into her house to get your juice. It was like you felt right at home. We were very proud of you. Later, you asked to go to Ashley's house again.

World news...Hurricane Katrina struck down on Louisiana (especially Greater New Orleans), Mississippi, Alabama, Florida Panhandle, most of eastern North America, Louisiana, on August 29, 2005, killing about 1,302 people. It had whipped the entire town out. Almost all the houses were covered up to rooflines. Katrina had become a category 5 with winds of 175 mph. People were left homeless and had to be evacuated from their own homes because it was unsafe. At least six people among a total of thirty people died after being infected by the vibrio bacteria in Louisiana, Alabama, and Mississippi.

People were evacuated to the Superdome in Texas. With no air-conditioning and little electricity, the heat and stench inside the Superdome were unbearable for the nearly twenty-five thousand housed there. As the water pressure lowered, toilets backed up. The stink was so bad that many medical workers wore masks as they walked around.

Consumers who were already juggling their budgets due to the higher cost of gasoline had to contend last month with prices that soared past $3 a gallon. And the two hurricanes, particularly Katrina, have led to hundreds of thousands of job losses, making people across the country uneasy about the economy.

I just wanted to let you know about this major event that happened during your lifetime. I love you so very much, and I am very thankful that you and sissy are in my life.

Love,
Mom

December 15, 2005

Dear Kendall,

You are a great big sister. You try to help Kasi all the time. You want to feed her, give her a bottle, try to change her diaper, and get her dressed. You even pick her up and carry her more than I'd like you to. Today you picked her up and accidentally bumped her head on the doorknob and gave her a knot above her eye.

Mommy and Daddy went to a Christmas dinner party last night. You and Kasi stayed the night at Grandma's house. While you were over at Grandma's, Santa Claus called and talked to you. He asked if you had been a good girl and asked you what you wanted for Christmas. You told him that you wanted doctor toys. You've really been into doctor toys lately. I bet you that Santa Claus will bring you some doctor toys for Christmas because you are such a good girl.

We went to Ella's, your friend from school, birthday party, and she received doctor stuff for her birthday. I'm thinking that's where the doctor toy idea came from. Ella is one of the little girls that you play with at school. You gave her the nickname Ella Honey. That's what you call her when you are playing with her. "Come here, Ella Honey. Ella Honey, come here."

You told Daddy and me the other day that you wanted to write a letter to Santa Claus this year. I'm going to help you write it and send it.

Funny Kendall moments:

You were playing at Grandma's, and you were both being funny. She said something to you, which I guess you didn't think was funny, and you were trying to be serious. You turned to Grandma and said, "Grandma, I'm not kidding."

You were playing. Grandma was the baby, and Kendall was Mommy. You said, "I have a deal for you. You lay down and I read you books." Grandma was not listening, and you said, "You have two choices. Mommy could go, or Mommy can stay. You choose." Grandma started to talk, and you cut her off, saying, "Mommy is going."

You were playing and running around one night, and you stopped to catch your breath. You said, "I like to run. It feels good. It makes my heart feel better."

When you don't listen to Mommy, I put you in a time-out. I usually sit you on the stairs for three minutes. After your time is up, I sit down next to you and ask you why you were put into time-out. I make you apologize, and then you give me a hug and a kiss. You were playing with Daddy one night, and you would act out exactly how and what I did when I put you into time-outs. You put Daddy into time-out about seven times. Each time, it was for something different. One time you had said that he was in time-out for talking to loud and being mean to sissy.

You were playing with Mommy's portfolio, and Daddy told you not to. You said, "Let me check my calendar" and held it like a book.

Daddy was saying something to you when you stopped what you were doing and turned toward him and said, "Just hush."

You are doing a lot in school. You have a lot of friends and enjoy your teachers. We went to a baby shower for one of you and Kasi's teachers the other day. You were, of course, the center of attention. You helped grab the presents and throw the wrapping paper away. You were such a great helper!

I was home with just you and Kasi one night, and Kasi was fussy. I was trying to get you and her some food at the same time. I was getting frustrated, and I had spilled a couple of things on the floor. You came over and helped me to pick up the food I had spilled onto the floor. After I changed Kasi's diaper, you threw it in the trash for me. You really are turning out to help more and more around the house. It's nice having that extra help. Thank you, baby girl, for being such a good helper and big sister.

I wanted to spend some alone time with you after Kasi went to bed the other night. I got out a bowl of water, lotion, and some nail polish, and we gave each other manicures and pedicures. You did well too. You didn't get any polish on my fingers themselves. You didn't cover the entire nail, but you did well. It was fun.

Mommy started a new job this week. It's very challenging and hard to learn, but I'm doing well. I'm working for a public relations firm. They write stories about different companies, people, events, and promotions that happen around Lake Tahoe. I sure hope it gets easier though.

Daddy has vacation time right now. He is off work for the next three weeks. You and Kasi are staying home with Daddy while I'm at work. I think it will be good for all of you. I think that you and sissy will challenge him and keep him on his toes.

I love you very much.

Love,
Mom

December 23, 2005

Dear friends and family,

Can you believe what date I am writing this letter? I have never been this late before. I guess it's better to be late than not at all. I wouldn't want you all to miss out on what is going on with our family. Obviously, we're busy!

Kasandra is almost eight months old now. She already has six teeth on the top coming in and only two on the bottom. It looks funny. She looks like a tooth monster. She hasn't really started to crawl yet, but she's moving around somehow. She's VERY noisy. She talks, mumbles out loud like she's telling you a story. She lets you know if she doesn't like something either. When we feed her, if she doesn't like it, she locks her jaws and makes this weird sound to let you know. She loves school. She smiles when we take her in and she sees her two favorite teachers. One of the teachers even has a nickname for her, Dinkam. I'm not quite sure what it means, but she lights up when she hears it. She's very sociable and loves people. We took the kids to see Santa Claus, and she cried when we put her on his lap. I think the beard thing scared her. When the cats walk by, she sounds like she's talking to them and grabs at them. She LOVES her big sister too. They are very good together.

Kendall is growing so fast. She seems like a five-year-old on some days, and then others, tantrum days, she seems two. She has two personalities. She has days where she really likes school, and then other days, she doesn't want to go and throws a fit. Kendall has quite a selection of friends at school. She's popular amongst the class. She has one friend named Ella, but she calls her Ella Honey. It's cute, too, because Ella is younger than her. "Ella Honey, come here, Ella Honey." She's good with Kasi. She tries to carry her around the house all the time. She treats her like a doll sometimes. She really loves her sister. She hugs and kisses her all the time. She's very protective of her too. We were doing laundry the other day, and two other kids came up to Kasi to talk to her. Kendall said, "That's my sister." When Art picks on Kasi, Kendall tells him to be nice to her baby and not to treat her like that. He's not mean to her. It's like when he pinches her cheek and she's tired, she'll start crying, and Kendall lets him have it. This year, for Christmas, she wanted doctor toys. That's really the thing she wanted. I don't know where she got the idea, but Santa is going to bring her some doctor toys. I'm sure that Kasi will be her patient.

Art is doing well. He's still working at the community college in the English as a Second Language Department. He's trying to recruit people to take more English classes. He's doing very well too. They liked him so much at the college that they agreed to change his schedule to fit our family needs and gave him a raise. He was working nights, and now he's able to be home with the family more, which is a huge help to the girls and me. It's been hard alone at night having to attend to Kasi and Kendall needing some attention. He and Kendall are growing closer to each other. She always wants Daddy to play with her. He's joined the Boys and Girls Club Board. He was on the Leadership of Lake Tahoe for about a year, which is a group of bigwigs from the area. He's doing a lot at the college as well. He's making a name for himself here in Lake Tahoe. He knows almost more people than I do now, and I've lived here my whole life. He's also taking college courses online and trying to finish his bachelor's in counseling. He stays very busy.

I have now moved onto another job. I was doing graphic design and marketing for a real estate firm, but they wouldn't help us to get a house, and so I quit. No, I'm kidding. I needed a change, and so now I'm working in a completely different field, media relations. I've been working here now for about two weeks, and already, I know that I made the right decision. The owner is great and flexible. I'm the office manager for a staff of five, and he's given me the okay to take everything over and run it. You gotta love that, right? Do whatever you have to do to run the show and get them organized. We are planning a conference called Operation Sierra Storm, and he has the former FEMA director, Michael D. Brown, coming to speak at the conference. It's a conference about weather and natural disasters. It's going to be huge. He helps run the PGA Tour and Celebrity Golf

Tournament every year. Lots of connections! Other than being busy with a new job, motherhood is still great YET CHALLENGING!

I hope you all have a great holiday!

Love,
Jeanna, Arturo, Kendall, and Kasandra

PS. There is another letter in here as well. That was the letter I tried to send around Kendall's birthday but was obviously never sent.

January 30, 2006

Dear Kendall Bug,

Today is Mommy's twenty-ninth birthday. Hard to believe that I'm that old already. I'll be thirty next year. Yikes! You're almost four years old. Time goes so fast.

I believe that you have a couple of imaginary friends now. You said the other day that you needed to call Norrisa, and you said her number was 544-7822. I mean, you said it like you called it all the time. You don't even know a Norrisa. I called the number, and it did not belong to anyone. I have no idea where you heard that name or that number.

Then you said that Marisa was sledding the other day. You don't know a Marisa either. I don't think you've ever heard those names before, so I guess you just made them up in your head.

You are doing better when you have to go to school now. Daddy said that he took you to school this morning, and you saw Avery, one of your friends from your class, and you just took off with her like Daddy wasn't even there. He said that he was leaving, and he did. You didn't even notice he was gone because you were too busy playing.

You received dress-up clothes and doctor toys for Christmas, and you've been playing with those a lot. You always want to listen to someone's heartbeat or check his or her temperature. You even check their ears and tell them that they have some sort of animal in their ears, like elephants.

Grandpa got you a couple pairs of doctor scrubs and a real stethoscope. He even got the hat and masks from the hospital that he works at. He also sent you a massaging, vibrating toy that you give massages with. Santa Claus brought you a doctor kit with a bag to hold everything.

Yesterday, I was not feeling well. I just wanted to lie down. You said that you wanted to play baby. I was the baby, and you were the mommy. You put a blanket over me and lay down next to me. You were even imitating me. You were telling me that Mommy would lie down with you, but only for a minute. You even scratched my back and arms. On the last arm, you told me that this was the last one. Meaning that this was the last thing to get scratched. You usually have me scratch both arms, your back, and your stomach. Depending on how tired I am though is how long I will scratch them for.

You have a new cartoon that you like now. It's called the *Little Einsteins*. It's a small group of kids that take adventures and explore in a little rocket. They have a classical musician and some famous artists that they focus on during the show. It really is very cute. It's my favorite one so far.

A couple days ago, we were driving in the car with Grandma, and someone almost pulled out in front of us. You said, "Hello, pain in the ass." Grandma and I were trying not to laugh because it was so funny and so off that we didn't know what else to do but laugh.

Another thing that was funny, and this was before my birthday came up. You said, "Mommy, I like your age." I said, "Well, that's good." I didn't know what else to say.

Grandma asked you if you wanted to play at her house one day, and you said, "Hold on. Let me check my schedule portfolio."

You are getting more dramatic in your storytelling now too. You were telling us a story. You were serious, waving your arms in front of your face. "It was getting darker and darker."

Daddy was bugging you the other day, and you told him, "Just hush." You seem to tell him that a lot. He bugs you a lot. I don't know who he bugs more, you or me, because he's bugging you and you come whine to me. When he bugs Kasi, you tell him that you don't like that and that she's your sister. You stick up for her all the time. Of course, Daddy still tries to irritate you though.

Yesterday, you came in from outside talking to Grandma about something, and you said, "The witch was totally mean."

You were being a stinker, and I must have said something or gave you a look. You said, "I'm not in trouble, am I? I'm cute, right?"

Kasi was rocking in a chair at Grandma's house, and she was whining. You said, "I know you're tired, Kasi. Just go to sleep. Someone's tired." And then you started to sing "Rock-a-Bye Baby."

You drew a picture and said, "This is for my Abuelita. She's my best friend." I think you got that from *The Wizard of Oz*. You've been watching some older movies lately—*Charlie and the Chocolate Factory*, *ET*, and *A Charlie Brown Christmas*.

I love you very much, my sweet baby.

Love,
Mom

March 24, 2006

Dear Kendall,

We had quit a scare this last month. I had a sharp pain in my side and went to the emergency room on February 20, only to find out that I had two ovarian cysts and one burst. That's what was causing me so much pain. Then on February 26, I took Kasi into the emergency room at 4:00 a.m. She had a high fever, 103°F. We had given her Tylenol and Motrin, but it was taking so long for her fever to go down. It finally went down, and they sent us home. Her fever went back up to 103.8°F, and we had been giving her both Tylenol and Motrin, alternating, and I was starting to get worried. There was a repertory virus, RSV, going around at the school where it was sending kids to the hospital because they were having problems breathing and had to be on oxygen. They didn't think she had it and still didn't know what it was. On February 28, we followed up at the doctor's office because she had a fever of 104.5°F the night before. The doctor sent her to the hospital just so that she could be monitored overnight. They did some tests on her and took a chest x-ray. She didn't have the RSV and no pneumonia. They never really found out what it was, but her fever went down in the hospital and stayed down. They thought it might have been either a bacterial infection or something viral, but they weren't exactly sure. It was scary though.

One night, she woke up crying and coughing. You told her, "Shhh, be quiet." It was sort of funny the way you said it. Like she was disturbing your sleep.

You stayed the night at Grandma's the night we stayed in the hospital. You told me the next day that you had a dream about Kasi and me in the hospital. I asked you if we were okay, and you said yes. I think you were worried about her in the hospital, especially after I was in the ER just a week prior. Too much is going on in one week if you ask me.

You and Kasi were playing together the other night, chasing each other around the house. You were both crawling. You would chase after her, and she would turn around to get you, and she was crawling as fast as she could to get away from you. It was the funniest thing. All three of us were laughing so hard. You even bonked heads a couple of times.

You were at Grandma's playing, and you told her that you wanted to be queen for a day.

You asked Grandma a question, and she didn't know what to say. You told Grandma to make up her mind.

You were trying to get Grandma to sit in your little rocking chair. She tried but couldn't fit. You told her that her butt was too big to fit in the rocking chair.

Grandma was talking to Cousin Kirsten on the phone. When she got off the phone, you asked her, "Who were you talking to? Your hunny bunny?"

You were watching a show at Grandma's about animals. You told her that the animals were strange and that they were gorgeous.

You were playing on the cell phone at Grandma's and talking to yourself one day. You said, "Stop it. You are embarrassing me." I say that to you when we are in a public place and you are being a stinker.

Grandma and I found out more information about an ingredient that was used in chewing gum that was very bad for you—aspartame. From now on, we look at the ingredients and try to find gum that has no aspartame. We were all at the store buying groceries, and you asked to get some gum. I was reading the back when you asked, "Mommy, does that one have aspartame?" That is a big word for you, but you said it perfectly. It threw Daddy and me both off. You are too smart for your own good sometimes.

I love you very much.

Love,
Mom

May 20, 2006

Dear Kendall Boom,

You are almost four years old, and your sissy is officially ONE YEAR old. It is so hard to believe that your sister is one year old already. It feels like we've reached a milestone with our family. Having two children is a lot of work. If one of you is crying, the other one needs something else. Sometimes I feel outnumbered with both of you needing something and I can't do both. It's starting to get a little bit easier knowing that your sister is getting older and a little more independent. Thank goodness.

On that note, we had her first birthday party. We had invited her little friend Anna and her brother, Noah. Noah is your friend from school, so you had a friend to play with as well.

You had a performance at school. It was Multicultural Day. The preschool room participates in the event by performing two little songs. Your sister's class came in their little buggy to watch. I took some pictures, of course. The video recorder was not working that day, so I didn't get to record it. You were a soccer player from Mexico. We made your hair in braids, and you wore your little soccer uniform. When you want your hair braided, you ask me to twist it. "I want them twisted." You did very well. I cried again. That's a mom for you. I was so proud of you.

The weather is starting to warm up now. We've all been trying to play outside more. You've been driving your Barbie car. We place both you and sissy in the car and drive around the neighborhood. We strap your sister in with Daddy's belt, like a seat belt, so that she doesn't fall out. It's really very cute, the two of you driving around in the little car. You must always stop and check to see if you have enough gas in your car. It's a battery-operated car.

On Mother's Day, we all went to Grandma's house and hung around there all day. We took your training wheels off your bicycle for the first time, and you did well. You were taking off and riding by yourself in no time. You were even going down the hills and across the little bridge by yourself. You only really fell once and scraped your arm a little teeny tiny bit. We were all so proud of you. The next couple of days, Grandma positioned sissy on the back of her bike while you rode your bike. You all went for a long bike ride.

Your sister is looking more like you. When she was a baby, she looked more like me. She has the same eye shape, same nose, and same lips and round-shaped face as you did when you were little. Really, the only obvious difference is the eye and hair color. You have brown eyes and brown hair. I think other people notice it more than we do though. Even your teachers say how similar you both look. I think because we see both of you every day, we don't notice as much. You are very stubborn though. Perhaps stubborn is not the right word to use, but strong-willed.

You are playing a lot of board games now. We've bought you a fishing game, Chutes and Ladders, a Winnie the Pooh matching game, Memory, Hungry Hippos, Break the Ice, and we've been playing Go Fish, Slap Jack, Uno, and Old Maid with cards. Sissy even plays Hungry Hippo and Break the Ice with us.

You were playing Go Fish with Grandma one day. Grandma asked if you had a card, and you said, "Of course I do, silly Grandma."

We were talking about colors the other night. You said, "I like blue, green, purple, pink, and orange. I don't like orange. Only sometimes I like orange."

You learned a song at school. "My mom's special. My mom's special. Look and see. Look and see. She loves me. She loves me. Lucky me. Lucky me." I thought this song was so cute.

I love you very much, and I am very proud of you. My little monkey.

Love,
Mommy

May 28, 2006

Dear Kendall,

We went on a bear hunt! A hunting we will go. A hunting we will go. High ho the dairy 'o. A hunting we will go.

Artists needed for "Bears by the Lake…a CeleBEARtion!"

"Bears by the Lake…a CeleBEARtion!" is a public art display and community fundraiser designed to help local youth-oriented organizations. The summer-long sightseeing campaign and fall auction is being organized by the LTVA, with the assistance of the 2005 Leadership Lake Tahoe class.

The campaign will feature 40–45 life-size fiberglass bear forms decorated by regional and local artists for public display throughout South Shore Lake Tahoe in "outdoor" galleries. The bears, dressed in brightly colored paints, creative mosaics and other artistic mediums, will stand 66" tall and weigh between 85 and 90 pounds. Some bears will be seated. Bear sighting maps will be distributed by the LTVA and local establishments to encourage self-guided sightseeing tours for bears from May 17 through Labor Day weekend in September. (www.recordcourier.com/news/2006/feb/27/artists-needed-for-bears-by-the-lake-a-celebeartio/)

We spent about eight hours or so in two days driving around to try and find all the bears and to take pictures. They are spread out from the shopping area at the "Y" to Zephyr Cove. You were starting to get good at spotting them too. "Mommy, look. There's another bear." They really are cool. I think they add character to the area, and it promotes the art in the area.

Just to name these few: Poppy Bear, Disco Ball Bear, Carmen Bearanda, Bogie Bear, Bear Your Soul, and the Pilot.

While we were driving in the car looking for bears, you started to sing a song to yourself in the back seat. "Lot-to ticket. Lot-to ticket. Here I am. Here I am. Lucky lotto ticket. Lucky lotto ticket. Here I am. Here I am." Daddy and I were laughing and asked you where you heard that song from. You said, "Grandma sings that song." That made us laugh even more. It was way too funny. We could picture Grandma singing that song too.

Driving in the car with Grandma, you had a toy cell phone in one hand like you were talking to someone and your purse wrapped around your other arm. You were talking on the phone, and then you started laughing. Grandma asked you what was so funny and who you were talking to. You said that you were talking to Ella Honey, and she said something funny to you. You were pretending because there was no one on the other line. Grandma said that you were carrying on this really long conversation like you were repeating an incident that happened at school.

You told Grandma that Ross loved you. I asked you, "How do you know that Ross loves you? Did he tell you?" You said, "He came up to me and said, 'Kendall, I love you.'" Grandma asked you if Ross was your boyfriend. You said yes.

When I came to pick you up from Grandma's house, you were playing morning news with your stuffed animals. You had your chalkboard, and the animals were all lined up in a row in front of you. You were asking them if anyone had any morning news. You would reply for them. "Yes, piggy. I went to abc.com with Logan." Then you would pretend to write it down on your chalkboard. You did that with all your animals, only each one had something different to say. You have morning news at school. You are disappointed now if you are late to school and you miss morning news.

Love,
Mom

June 22, 2006

Dear Kendall,

We went on a family trip to San Diego. All four of us flew on a plane together. We stayed at this hotel called Town and Country. The hotel and grounds were beautiful. The grounds were so large that we were given a ride to our room from the front desk to the room. The grounds were covered in flowers and roses. You could smell roses everywhere you turned. There were four swimming pools and I believe four restaurants on the grounds as well. There was a mall within walking distance behind the hotel which we walked over to. We had to buy your shoes because we forgot to pack some for you. We stayed there for three nights and four days while Daddy went to a conference for one day.

We spent a day in Old Town State Historic Park in San Diego. We took a tram, which was about a ten-minute ride. The park includes a main plaza, exhibits, museums, restaurants, and shops.

We all spent a day at Sea World. We rented a double stroller so in case you or Kasi got tired, you could sleep, and we wouldn't have to carry you all day. We tried to see every show and every ride. You and I went on a water ride, *Shipwreck Rapids*, and you absolutely loved it. I told you in advance that you were going to get wet, and you were getting excited. We only got a little wet though. You wanted to go again with Daddy, but while we were on the ride, they had to stop it to save a seagull that was in danger from part of the ride. We had to be escorted off our boat, and they closed the ride until someone came to get the bird. He could not fly because his wings were wet.

Wild Arctic is an attraction where we were face-to-face with a polar bear that was sleeping, beluga whales, walruses, arctic foxes, and seals.

Just outside the attraction was an area of penguins swimming and walking around in a pool.

Journey to Atlantis, a water coaster, was another wet ride that we went on. You and Daddy went on it first while I stayed with Kasi to watch you come out. When you came down from the ride, you wanted to go again, and so I went with you. During the ride, you were scared and then excited at another point. When we got off the ride, you wanted to go again. It started to get late, and we didn't want you to be cold if you got wet more than you already were. You were supposed to be over 42" tall to experience most of the rides, and you just barely made it. Good thing you're tall.

Cirque de la Mer was a performance on water combining mysterious creatures, acrobatics, music, and special effects. There were acrobats jumping from a swing into the water performing flips and summersaults in the air. There were a few people on swings and ropes. They even had fireworks at the end of the show.

Clyde and Seamore's Risky Rescue was a show of two seals and a walrus that performed a comedy show of attractions. It was cute.

Believe, a captivating and visually stunning new Shamu show. We saw this show twice because it was so good. Shamu and a few other whales performed with flips and jumps. They danced and worked with trainers shooting them up in the air on their noses. The whales would swim near the audience and get them all wet by spraying them with water. This was your favorite show. We even brought home a baby Shamu stuffed toy for both you and Kasi. Kasi was even clapping at the end of the performance.

You were able to hold a live starfish in a water cavern. We tried to touch stingrays as well, but it was hard to reach them. We watched guests working with dolphins one-on-one.

It was a very long day, and we still had to get back to the hotel. We were all very tired and hungry. It took us a couple of days to catch with some energy because we did so much all week long. We all had a great time though.

On the flight home, we flew back with Conner, who is in your class at school. You wanted to sit next to him on the plane, and you did for a little bit, but then he wanted his mommy. You were very bummed and were upset that you couldn't play with him anymore. It was nice for you to have a friend on our trip for a short period.

Grandma left town the same night we came back from San Diego. She and Pam flew to the Dominican Republic. They are supposed to be gone for about ten days.

When Grandma returns from vacation, you are supposed to start swimming lessons again.

We are also putting you in soccer this year, and that is supposed to start mid-August.

We are going to be very busy this summer.

Love,
Mom

August 4, 2006

Dear Kendall,

Life has been so busy for all of us. Just recently, we decided to move. We found this three-bedroom, one-bathroom house with a fenced backyard and a washer/dryer. Heavenly! It will be so nice once we move into the new place. There will be a large backyard for you and Kasi to play in. We are going to be moving in about a week.

We still haven't had your fourth birthday party either. We were originally going to have a Dora the Explorer party at Kahle Community Center, but now that we will have a house and yard, I think we will have a pool party instead at the house. You did have a small party at your school the day of your birthday though. All the kids sang happy birthday, and I brought homemade cupcakes.

We went to the park one night a couple of weeks ago, and it was sort of chilly out. We were playing on the swings when you shouted out, "My hands are fucking cold!" My mouth dropped. I couldn't believe what I just heard came out of your mouth. Daddy and I both had a talk with you about that not being a very nice word and that you should never say it again. I still can't believe you said that word.

Another day, we were riding in the car talking. I don't even remember what it was exactly that we were talking about, but you said something like, "Oh shit, I forgot." Again, I told you that word was not a nice word and that you should not use that word again. I know that you hear these words from Mommy, Daddy, and Grandma, and we shouldn't say them either. We need to watch our own mouths.

You've been sick lately. You were running a fever for about four to five days. One day, it was 104°F. We were alternating Tylenol and Motrin to try and control your temperature. We even had your head wrapped up in cold wet washcloths to try and keep your temperature down. You threw up the medicine a few times. You were barely keeping anything in your stomach. A couple days into it, you were complaining of a stomach pain in your right side. We thought that it might be your appendix. Then the pain moved over to the left side.

We thought perhaps your stomach muscles were sore from all the vomiting.

You had a large bug bite on the top of your right foot. There was a case of West Nile virus in Carson City, a half hour away from us. We thought you might have that.

West Nile Virus in Illinois—Surveillance

Neuroinvasive Disease. The most severe type of disease due to a person being infected with West Nile virus is sometimes called "neuroinvasive disease" because it affects a person's nervous system. Specific types of neuroinvasive disease include: West Nile encephalitis, West Nile meningitis or West Nile meningoencephalitis. Encephalitis refers to an inflammation of the brain, meningitis is an inflammation of the membrane around the brain and the spinal cord, and meningoencephalitis refers to inflammation of the brain and the membrane surrounding it.

West Nile fever. West Nile Fever is another type of illness that can occur in people who become infected with the virus. It is characterized by fever, headache, tiredness, aches and sometimes rash. Although the illness can be as short as a few days, even healthy people have been sick for several weeks.

Other Clinical/Unspecified. Includes persons with clinical manifestations other than West Nile fever, West Nile encephalitis or West Nile meningitis, such as acute flaccid paralysis. Unspecified cases are those for which sufficient clinical information was not provided. (www. idph.state.il.us/envhealth/wnvcounty/wnvla- salle05.htm)

104

The pain moved down to the inside of your right inner thigh. The doctor took a urine specimen and found blood and crystals, which are possible signs of a kidney stone. They did one more test for a urinary tract infection, and that wasn't it. The doctor saw you again and said the lump on the inside of your leg was a lymph node. You are just a lumpy kid. You've also had lymph nodes on the top of your head and the side of your neck. It's always something new. We still don't really know what was going on, but you are doing much better. The doctor thinks that you have a virus or something, and we just must let it pass. You still have a little pain in the inner right thigh, but you are doing much better.

You were part of a bike-a-thon at school. The school was helping to raise money for St. Jude Children's Hospital. People donated money for how many laps you went around or just a flat donation. You and Kasi both did it, and you received a T-shirt for participating. You really enjoyed that day at school. After the bike-a-thon, they had a magician come to perform in front of your class. The magic word was *abracadabra*.

I love you very much.

Love,
Mom

October 30, 2006

Dear Kendall,

We finally had your birthday this weekend! There has been so much going on that it seemed like it was never going to happen.

We finally moved, and then a couple weeks later, I lost my job, and so the money was tight. I told Daddy that we needed to have a party for you before Christmas though. Money was still tight, but we didn't want you to feel that we forgot. We decided to have a Halloween-themed party. You had never had one of those before, and so it was going to be different.

We scheduled your party the weekend before Halloween. We decorated the house with a big spider and spiderweb in the living room. We had ghosts and bats hanging from the ceiling as well as some pumpkins. We even got a Mrs. Potato Head pumpkin dress-up kit for your pumpkin.

I had planned to have a couple crafts: decorate pumpkins with construction paper (either a princess or a bat). We also made spider bracelets. I found a picture off the internet of Casper the Ghost and Wendy the Good Witch on a flying broom. I made a "pin the broom on the witch" game. You helped me paint the brooms for all your friends. We also bought the movie *Casper the Ghost* and watched part of that as well.

For the gift bags, I didn't want to hand out any candy since it was so close to Halloween, so we gave the trick-or-treat bags with a Halloween book, mini pumpkin, bat rings, Halloween rattles, pumpkin Frisbees, and Halloween plates that we used for the food and cake were plastic reuseable plates that we gave them to take home as well. The only sugar was the Oreo cookie ice cream cake that was decorated as a pumpkin.

The party went great! Your friends that came in costume were Ella, Ross, Katherine, Emarie, and Avery. We also invited Allon, Noah, Anna, Mateo, and Taylor, but they were not able to make it. For your presents, you received dress-up clothes, a dress-up mirror, pajamas, a Dora book, bubble bath, a Strawberry Shortcake doll, and an Ariel doll.

Since I've been so busy with trying to find a job, I've also been working at your school to help. I move about to all three rooms—infant, toddler, and the preschool room. I haven't made the time to write to you much in the last month. I did write some things down though.

One night, we had asparagus for dinner. You don't really like asparagus very much. I was trying to make you eat just a few bits, and then you said that it was hurting your tongue. You said that you couldn't eat asparagus because you were allergic to it. You even stuck out your tongue and showed me.

I was giving Grandma a hard time for the way she was parking in the dip of the driveway one day. She said that she parked in the dip. I told her that she was a dip. You looked at both of us and told us that we were both dips. Grandma and I both laughed.

I took you out for a bike ride around our new neighborhood, and on our way home, it was getting darker. You were behind me, and all of a sudden, I heard this crash, and you were crying. I turned around to see what had happened, and you had run your bike into the back of a parked car. You crashed. It was so funny. You were crying, and I was laughing. I still don't know how you could run into a parked car.

You played soccer well. At first, you were not really excited about it. During a game, you and another girl were playing with each other's hair when the other team ran by you with the ball and scored a goal. Daddy and I told you that if you scored a goal, we would buy you a present, thinking that would motivate you. It sure did too. You were the most improved player. You scored almost two goals in every game after that. You did so well that we bought you a CD Walkman player. We were so proud of you. Soccer is over now, and you received a trophy for playing.

I took you fishing over at the Trout Farm. It was the first time you had caught a real fish. I took you over to watch first to see what was involved, and that's when you decided you wanted to do it too. We drove back home and got Daddy and Kasi. I helped you place the bait on the hook, and you held the pole. As soon as the fish was hooked on it, I took the pole. I pulled the fish out, and you put him in the net. You were so proud of yourself for catching a fish. We caught two and took them home for dinner. They were good too.

You and baby were playing together one day. I had walked out of the room, and I heard you telling Kasi, "Baby, when Mommy is not around, you need to listen to my words." You try to boss her around sometimes. She can be bossy herself though.

We were at the grocery store for something, and you were in the front of the cart facing away from me. I took some gum off the shelf and put it behind me on the counter. When we walked outside, you asked me for some gum. I told you that I didn't have any. You said, "Yes, you do. It's in the bag." I couldn't believe you saw me buy the gum. You are so sneaky.

Daddy had a salon day with you, and you were painting each other's nails. First you painted Daddy's feet and hands, and then he painted yours. You told Daddy that he looked like a big strong Daddy now with his nails painted. When he missed a spot on your nails, you would let him know that he was not doing a very good job and that you did better than him.

You tend to read books to your babies when you are playing. You wanted to read a story to me. You started to tell me a story, and then you said, "Banana Republic." I asked you where you heard those words. You said, "The TV." Banana Republic is a name-brand clothing line.

I asked you how your day went at school. I asked whom you played with, and I named a few people. I mentioned a girl named Anna. You told me, "Sometimes I don't feel like playing with Anna, and sometimes I do. Sometimes I don't like being silly. Sometimes I like being an adult."

Kasi tends to wake up in the morning before you, and she'll wake you up. She was awake one morning, making a lot of noise. You told her, "Shh, I've heard enough already."

You and Kasi were playing dress-up one night, and she just sat still while you put clips in her hair and put shoes on her feet. You put about six different pairs of shoes on her feet. You both play very well together most of the time. I'm so glad.

Since soccer is over, we thought we would let you try something else. You really wanted to do gymnastics, but you also wanted to dance all the time. Tonight, I took you to try out a dance class with Ella. You were so excited and did very well. After the class, you decided that you wanted to take dancing instead of gymnastics. You wore a little pink tutu.

I love you very much. You are my little princess.

Love,
Mom

December 4, 2006

Dear Kendall,

It's getting closer to Christmas as there are some holiday things happening. Last weekend, we took you and Kasi to Santa at the Village. It was an event being put together at the Heavenly Village stores. We took you and Kasi to see Santa Claus and get your pictures taken on his lap and to let him know what you wanted for Christmas. You sat on his lap all by yourself this year. You did very well. You sat on his lap and talked to him. You told him that you wanted a real kitchen and a scooter. Kasi, on the other hand, was terrified of him. The moment we put her on Santa's lap, she was screaming. We even got a picture of her screaming and you sitting there very calmly.

You also walked up to Frosty the Snowman and gave him a hug. Kasi again was terrified. She was shaking and saying no before we even walked up to him.

We saw Rudolph the Red-Nosed Reindeer. You gave him a hug as well. We went to get your faces painted, and you decided to get a reindeer. After your face was painted, you wanted to go back and show Rudolph and give him another hug. It was very sweet. There was also a polar bear that you hugged.

You both received ornaments with your names on them. You received a penguin animal from Mrs. Claus, you made a cookie, and we watched a few ice-skaters perform. It was a very nice day.

I think we brought home a different child that afternoon though. We brought home the not so good Kendall. You had climbed behind the Christmas tree to hide, and I believe that you got stuck back there, afraid that you were going to knock the tree over. You peed in your pants. You came out from behind the tree, just soaked. We were so mad at you. We gave you a couple choices for your punishment: you could not stay the night at Grandma's house that night, no books for a week, or no TV and computer for a week. You decided not to have the books.

The next morning, you peed in your pants again. You even lied to try and hide it. You told Grandma that you didn't poop, but you did. When she asked to check to see if you wiped good or not, she discovered your pants were wet. I gave you another punishment—no TV or computer or no dance class. So now you have been without TV, computer, and books for a week. We told you that if peed in your pants again, you would have to wear diapers again. I hope that you quit peeing in your pants. This is hard.

On to other happenings. You have a crush on the teacher's aide in your classroom. His name is Arthur, and he's twenty-two years old. You still don't really talk to any of your teachers in class, but Arthur is another story. You play roughhouse with him. You try to beat him up. You talk about him when you come home. When I ask you what you did at school, you usually say something about Arthur. "Arthur took my shoe away from me today." I caught you hugging him the other day. It's funny. We call Arthur your boyfriend.

Your birthday party went well. All your friends came over and played with your toys. No one really wanted to do the activities I had planned other than pin the broom on the witch, and no one really wanted to watch *Casper*, but you had fun.

You went trick-or-treating with Katherine and Kelsey Jean on Halloween night. You had fun, but I was not happy with the way that Katherine treated you and Kelsey. She was mean to the both of you. There were a couple of times that she made Kelsey cry, and you tried to comfort Kelsey and included her. You were very sweet. I was very proud of you.

You are really doing well in your ballet class. Not only is Ella in the class, but Macy, Olivia, and Lexy are in the class as well. The class has been skipping from one side of the room to the other, and at first you were the only one who knew how to skip. I was very proud of you. You are really into this class. I think we are going to keep you in this class for another six months or so. There is a performance at the end of the season. I can hardly wait for that.

We went to Los Angeles over another holiday weekend. This time, Kasi and I went with you and Daddy. While we were sitting in traffic, Daddy and I were talking about an old car that Daddy had when he lived in Los Angeles. We were arguing about the color of the car being blue or brown when suddenly, you say, "You guys, stop. Daddy's car is red." His current car is red. It was so funny.

Daddy always picks on you, and sometimes he will pick on you until you cry. You tell me a lot that you love me. "Mommy, I love you." I love it when you say that. Daddy asked you if you loved him. You said, "I love you only when you don't pick on me."

Daddy was picking on Kasi and almost made her cry. You told him, "How dare you talk to my baby like that." You defend her a lot when it comes to Daddy.

You've been practicing your handwriting and spelling your name on your own. You've even been practicing writing your friends' names. You are good at writing their names too.

Ella has a brother, Mateo, as well as Mom and Dad. Ella always wants to play Mom, Dad, Sister, Brother. Like playing house. You used to play baby a lot. You would be the mom, and someone else, usually Daddy or Grandma, would play with the baby. You heard Ella say that she wanted to play Mom, Dad, Sister, Brother the other day, and you said it just the same. Daddy asked what you wanted to play, and you said, "I want to play Mom, Dad, Sister, Brother."

I sat Kasi on the toilet the other day to see if she would use the potty. She didn't, but I was telling someone else about it, and you were listening. You said, "Aww, little Kasi is potty training."

Your coloring has been getting better. You've been paying more attention to coloring in the lines.

You can now say our phone number, 544-2978, as well as Grandma's, 544-7376, and dial them on your own. You were over at Grandma's the other day, and you called and left about five messages on the answering machine for me.

We started putting a lock on the dried feed cabinet for Kasi to stay out. Instead of eating dinner, she will get down and head straight for the goldfish or something like it. Kasi was pulling Tupperware out of the cabinet when you told her to stop. She made some noise back at you. You said, "Do we have to put a lock here too?" Okay, little miss bossy.

You and Kasi were taking a bath together one night. You pointed at her and said, "Look, Kasi has baby-sized chi chis, and I have Kendall-sized chi chis."

I had to put Abby to sleep the day before Thanksgiving. She was getting sick and thin. The doctor said that her kidneys were not so good. You've been having a hard time with it. You mentioned that we needed a new cat for Motita. You said that she would be very lonely when we went out of town and that she needed someone there to keep her company. You even asked if Abby was not going to sleep with you in your bed anymore. I don't know if you really understand or not, but you still question it all. She was seventeen years old and lived a great life. We all loved her and miss her.

Love,
Mom

December 6, 2006

Dear friends and family,

Is there ever a time a year that your family is not busy? I feel like I'm always on the go. When is it my time to rest?

The holidays are here again. I really do like this time of year. It reminds me what important things I must do—spend time with my family and enjoy it. I did not have a chance to write a midyear letter again this year. A lot has been happening.

I started working for the community college in the girls' school for someone who was out on maternity leave. I really liked it, but it's only part-time until the girl comes back from maternity leave.

I was then hired on at the college foundation department. The most recent event that I have helped with is trying to acquire some donations in helping our local elementary schools with coats for kids. We are giving children that are less fortunate than us a chance to stay warm for the winter season.

I had surgery in September as well. I had a hysterectomy. During the surgery, they found a tumor on one ovary, and it turned out not to be cancerous. They ended up taking my other ovary out altogether. They left one in for the hormones. I feel much better now. I had endometriosis. It's a disease that forms blood clots on the inside of your female organs. I had two previous surgeries to get it under control, but they did not help. That is why I had the hysterectomy. We have two beautiful girls. We are grateful for what we have.

Kendall is almost five years old. Her personality is starting to shine a little more now that Kasi is around. She is not as shy. She played soccer this last season and did well. At first, she was not really into it. We told her that if she scored a goal, we would buy her a present. The next games, she said that she was going to score six goals. Art and I thought we were in for our money. She scored two goals, and from then on, she tried hard. She was the most improved player on the team. Everyone on the team received a little trophy for his or her achievement. She was so proud of it. She wanted to show it to everyone.

We asked her what she wanted to do next since soccer was over. She could choose between gymnastics or dance. I took her to a dance class, and she was so excited that we joined the next day. She's in beginning ballet. She was so into it that it was like she had always been there. She's even a little more advanced than some of the girls that had been there from the start. Two months' difference. She will have her dance performance in June.

She's learned our phone number as well as Grandma's. I came home the other day to hear six messages from her. She was testing out her phone skills. She didn't really talk too much, but now she calls both numbers all the time. She and Kasi stayed the night at Mom's the other night, and she called me at 7:30 a.m. to invite me over to Grandma's for breakfast. Then she asked if I wanted to sleep in. I couldn't go back to sleep.

Kendall will be starting kindergarten next fall. I am so nervous about this. Where is the parents' manual for this one?

Kendall has a crush on this guy in her class. Yes, guy. He's the teacher's aide, and he's twenty-two years old. It's funny. She does not talk to most of the teachers at the school, but she talks to him all the time. He picks on her the most though. He'll tease her and take her shoes and hang her upside down. Whatever he can to torture her. I found her giving him a hug the other day. It really is funny to watch.

A few things that she's said. Art always picks on her, and sometimes he will pick on her until she cries. She tells me a lot that she loves me. "Mommy, I love you." I love it when she says that. Art asked her if she loved him. She said, "I love you only when you don't pick on me."

Art was picking on Kasi and almost made her cry. She told him, "How dare you talk to my baby like that." She defends her a lot when it comes to Daddy.

Kasi is nineteen months and talking up a storm. She tries to repeat everything we say. With her own little twist, of course. She's funny when she plays peekaboo, only she says peet-boo. She understands some Spanish. Art talks to her only in Spanish.

Kasi is a lot more outgoing and has a vibrant personality. You don't want to make her mad though. She gets mean and says no very sternly. She knows what she likes and doesn't like. She's very sociable. When we are out in public, she says hi to almost everyone.

Kasi and Kendall look alike in their features, but Kasi is blond and has blue eyes like Mom. She looks like a little Jeanna.

We took the girls to see Santa Claus already, and Kasi screamed as soon as we put her on Santa's lap. Kendall, for the first time, sat on his lap and told him what she wanted for Christmas—a real kitchen play set and a motorized scooter. Grandma found a motorized Harley-Davidson scooter that she wanted to get Kendall instead. I'm not so happy about that. Kendall has a twenty-two-year-old boyfriend and a Harley-Davidson at age of four and a half years old. See why we are busy?

Art is still working for the college as well. He's very much a valued part of the college. He thinks he walks on water here and can do nothing wrong. They really like him and played a key role here.

Art is almost done with getting his bachelor's degree. He's been taking classes online and has about a year or so left. I'll be so glad when this is over. We'll have more time with him.

He is having his citizenship ceremony on December 21. This means that he will be a US citizen now. He's very nervous. It has been a very long process. About five years' worth.

I hope you all have a great holiday season. Enjoy each other as well.

Love,
Jeanna, Arturo, Kendall, and Kasandra

February 18, 2007

Dear Kendall,

Every now and then, you go through phases with Kasi. Yesterday, you were mean to her all day. You didn't want to share anything with her. You wouldn't let her play with you, and you were too rough with her.

Today, you awoke a new child. You shared your Cheerios with her. You went to the refrigerator and grabbed her drink. You opened the refrigerator for her to put her cup away when you were both done eating. You wanted to play and dance with her.

Sometimes you are good to her, and other days you can be just so mean to her. Since Kasi does not know how to verbalize enough to you, sometimes she bites. You were being a little rough with her today, and she said no. You didn't stop, and she bit you on the side of your face. It made you cry, and you let her go. This has happened a few times. You just don't know your limits with her sometimes.

You went to Emarie's birthday party yesterday. Katherine, Kelsey, and Avery were there as well. It didn't go over that well. You were all fighting and making each other cry. You were the nicest of them all. One of them called you poophead and made you upset. Some of your friends are not very nice. I hope that you don't grow up to be mean like your friends.

You play well with Ella. You always say that she's your best friend. You've had many playdates with her, and you both get along well for the most part. I like it when you play with her.

Even in dance class, you are connected. Sometimes we wonder if you sat close enough to each other, you'd become one person. You are always right next to each other. Practically sitting on top of each other. They gave you leg warmers and ballet socks so that the two of you will match. You're the only two in class that have leg warmers.

Just to catch up on a few things that have happened as well.

You wrote a letter to Santa this year. I asked you what you wanted to say, and then I told you what letters to write. You wrote:

> Dear Santa, I love you. Santa, I want a pur-
> ple skirt for me. A blue skirt for baby. A Harley,
> a real kitchen.

It was so very cute. I made copies of it and mailed them with our annual Christmas letter to all our friends and family.

We were shopping near Christmastime, and we were buying you some pants. We were standing in line to pay when you saw a picture of a slushy on the counter. You said that you really wanted one. I mentioned that you were already getting pants and that you didn't need sugar, specifically overalls. You really like overalls. I gave you the option to put the pants back if you wanted the slushy. You chose the slushy and said, "Santa will bring me a pair of overalls." I told you that he was already bringing you something else that you had asked for. The real kitchen. You did not get a slushy.

Daddy had received notice that he had been granted his citizenship right before Christmas. We drove down to Sacramento to attend the ceremony. It was raining hard down in Sacramento, and so we didn't stay long down there. As soon as it was over, we drove home. It was snowing on top of the hill as we were driving home. The 4x4 was not working great on the car, and we were stuck on a hill. Every time we tried to adjust the tires, we would slide back a little closer to the edge of the road, which had a cliff on the other side. It was very scary. Someone in a road vehicle came by to see if we were okay and said he would send someone to come and help us. We waited for a couple of hours, and no one came. We were tired and running out of food and water. We were all cold and scared. Finally, I got out of the car and flagged someone down on the side of the road. They had cell phones that reached for help. Someone was coming to help us, but they said that it might be four hours before they made it to us. We called Grandma and asked her to come and get you and Kasi while Daddy and I took care of the car. The tow truck came before Grandma did, and we passed her on the way to come and get you. We made it home safely! I was still worried about Grandma though. We hadn't heard from her about whether she was home or not yet. An hour had passed when she drove up to the house. She was fine as well. That was the scariest feeling in my life. We thought that we were not going to make it home that night. You were very scared as well.

You were going to Grandma's work with her one night. You were wearing a Barbie sweatshirt. You said, "I think everyone is going to love my Barbie shirt."

You and Kasi were at Grandma's for the day, and you came home starving. I asked you if Grandma made you any lunch. You said no. I asked Grandma, and she said that she forgot. A couple of days later, you told Grandma that you were hungry. You said that Grandma feeds you, but Mommy doesn't. Which I thought was funny since Grandma was the one who forgot to feed you, not me.

You have been pushing me away lately. It hurts my feelings. I cried a few times. You were coming home from wherever it was and not talking to me at all. You went to Los Angeles with Daddy for four days, and you didn't say one word to me when you walked in the door. One night, when you hadn't said a word to me, you came up to me and asked me for my help on something. I told you that if you were not going to talk to me, that you could go ask Daddy for help. I was not going to help you until you said hi to me. You paused and said, "Hi, Mommy, can you help me?"

I sat you down one night and talked to you about ignoring me. I told you that I was going to start ignoring you to let you know how it felt and that it was very upsetting to me. You were hurting my feelings. I think you understood me because after I talked to you, you changed your attitude.

For my birthday this year, I turned thirty years old. I really was having a hard time with turning thirty. I wanted to spend the day with you at the salon since the ignoring me part was bothering me so much. I am not looking forward to you growing up and apart from me as you become more independent. It makes me very sad just thinking about it.

It was Grandma, you, and me. We had our hair done first. The stylist washed and dried your hair and curled and styled it. It looked cute on you.

Then we went upstairs to the nail studio to get our nails and toes cleaned up and painted. You were relaxed. You looked like you were going to fall asleep while they were doing your feet. You had a good time, and you were a very good girl. That was my birthday present to myself—spending time with you, just like girls.

One night, you were being a stinky. Okay, you are a stinker a lot of the time, but this night was unforgettable. You ran upstairs to get some clothes for bed and stuck your butt up against the heater while you were naked to warm your butt, only you burnt it. You had a mark on both cheeks from the heater. It looked like a grill mark on your butt. I couldn't help but laugh, but you did a pretty good number on yourself.

You've been getting better about letting Daddy read books to you at night. You've even become more tolerable when there is only one of us putting you and Kasi to sleep. You're more patient. You're even sleeping in a little longer now. You usually roll over and tell Kasi to be quiet so that you can get more sleep.

I hope that as you get older, we stay very close. I love you very much and want you to know that *no matter what*, I will always love you. Even if you turn into a swishy bug. I will still love you and give you a hug. You are still my baby girl, and I love spending time with you.

Love,
Mom

March 26, 2007

Dear Kendall,

You have been trying to go to bed without diapers on, and there are some nights that you make it through the night and other nights that you have accidents. I don't know exactly if you are waking up and peeing in your bed or if you wake up from peeing in your sleep. It does not happen all the time. We give you a hard time, telling you that Kasi will be out of diapers before you. Kasi has been using the potty more. She says that she must go potty before she goes in her diaper.

Daddy was working late when I took you and Kasi to the new Taco Bell. I ordered your original order of one hard and one soft taco with meat, cheese, and sour cream. Normally, you have just one taco each, but for some reason, you wanted four tacos. You ate all four of them too. I couldn't believe how many tacos you had.

Kasi has been talking more. She's been saying enough words to make sentences. We had been counting how many words she was saying. For example, she said, "You're welcome." These really are two words, right? You were trying to figure it out on your fingers, and instead of counting the words, you were counting the syllables. You thought she was saying three words, but it was two words and three syllables. I was impressed that you were trying to understand words like this.

Grandma taught you how to blow a bubble with your tongue. I came home from work, and you were blowing bubbles for the rest of the day. Kasi kept trying to pop them once you blew one up.

We got a new playground for the backyard from a friend of the family, John Poell. They have a ten-year-old son that doesn't play with it anymore, and he gave it to us for free. It took us four hours to take it apart from his house and about twelve hours for us to put it back together. You and Kasi love it though. It features: a swing, teeter-totter, monkey bars, slide, picnic table, a climbing wall, rope climbing wall, ladder, and a roof over the top of the structure. You've already fallen from the monkey bars. You got tangled in the swing and teeter-totter trying to skip bars, and your hand slipped.

In dance class, ballet, you've been doing so well. You are the head person in class now. Your class was supposed to skip backwards across the room, and you did great. You also have a dance recital coming up in June, right before your birthday. Your costumes are ballerinas with lamb ears. You had your individual and group photos in your costumes done.

You had your first sleepover. You stayed the night over at your good friend Ella Hirschfield's house. You did very well. You even talked to her mom, Michelle. You were both very excited. You didn't even get scared. You also stayed up until about 11:00 p.m., laughing and giggling until Michelle came into the room and made you both quit playing.

You were playing over at Grandma's when you were playing with your babies. You were playing nap time with them. You would lay them down with pillows and cover them with blankets. Then you would sit down and rub their backs. Grandma asked if you needed any help with the babies. You said, "No, I can handle it."

We try to have family time and play some games altogether. We played board games with you and Kasi. Don't Wake Daddy. This is a board game where the first player tiptoes from your bed, past all the noisy obstacles, to the refrigerator for a midnight snack without waking Daddy. Land on a plain-colored space without a picture and number: You're safe! If you land on a space with a picture and number and you don't have a card that matches the space, you must push the button on the alarm clock the number of times indicated on the space. If you wake Daddy, he will pop up in bed! If Daddy sleeps through the alarm, stay in that space until your next turn. The first player to land on the Rainbow Refrigerator wins.

You also like to play Perfection. You've got to put all twenty-five different shapes into corresponding holes in the spring-loaded tray before the sixty-second timer runs out! When the clock clangs, the tray scatters pieces all over! Set a personal best time or challenge a friend to beat you. You'll quickly develop a strategy for speed! It's the perfect game for time-tickin' action. Store parts neatly with built-in storage tray. For one or more players. You are learning your shapes pretty good with this game. Not necessarily the names of them, but the pieces to the board game.

Don't Break the Ice can only be played with two people, but we take turns. The objective is to tap out the ice blocks one by one. They won't melt when you are done! Take your time and do some thinking. To keep the polar bear from sinking. To win, the bear must stay on top. One wrong block, he'll go ker-plop!

Pooh Musical Hide 'n Seek. The object is to press Pooh's head to play the music and make his friends peek out from their honeypots. Who's hiding in which pot?

To play, flip over a card and try to find the matching character. To win, match all six of your cards by finding all six of Pooh's friends: Piglet, Tigger, Eeyore, Rabbit, Owl, and Kanga!

Let's Go Fishin'. This is one of Kasi's favorites, but you get bored too easily with it. Each player has a separate fishing pole with plastic "bait" at the end of the line. As the fish open their mouths, carefully lower your line into the fish's mouth, catching it as it takes the bait!

One of your favorite games is Mouse Trap. This one has too many little pieces in it, and so we play this one when Kasi takes a nap. The object is to build a better mousetrap, and you can catch your opponent's mouse before yours is caught! As you travel around the board, collect pieces to create your trap, then put it together and start up the whole crazy chain reaction. This is no ordinary mousetrap! For two to four players. You really get into these games. The more you play them, the better you get.

You often stay the night at Grandma's house on her nights off from work. About a couple of weeks ago, Kasi would not let Grandma leave without her. Kasi ended up staying the night at Grandma's house too. It's only a matter of time before both of you go over and stay the night more often.

Kasi tries to copy you with a lot of things. You skip backwards, and then she tries. You did the wheel barrel in your dance class. When you came home from class, you tried it with Kasi, and she did it. This is where someone holds your legs and you walk on your hands. You must have strong arms for this, and you both do.

You, Kasi, Grandma, and I went to Santa Rosa for Kirsten's baby shower. It's about three and half hours away from home. You played with this little girl named Samantha, who is the same age as you.

You are chasing and kissing the boys at school. Apparently, you are not the only little girl doing this in your school either. You normally kiss Allon and Kaden. I don't really like this, but I guess it's normal for your age.

We went to an open house at the school where you will be starting kindergarten. You didn't really care about the school or the classrooms. You just wanted to play with some of the toys in the rooms. I really liked the school though. You also had an assessment test to see if you are ready to start kindergarten. The teacher said that you did well, but that you wrote your name backwards. I thought this was odd. You had never done this before.

Anyway, you are going to start in September. I'm getting nervous.

I sure do love you. I can't believe how fast you are growing.

Love,
Mommy

April 9, 2007

Dear Kendall,

Yet another eventful visit to the doctor's office. Your face had swollen up to the largest we have ever seen under your right ear. Your lymph nodes were so hard and putting pressure on your face that it was very painful for you. Before, when your face would swell up, the doctors would tell us that there was nothing we could do except alternate Tylenol and Motrin, unless it got to the point where it gave you an ear infection. Then they would give you amoxicillin.

This last time I took you in to see our normal family doctor, he felt that you should be seen by a specialist. Grandma took you to see the ear, nose, and throat specialist, Paul Manoukian, MD. And he wanted to get a CT scan of your face to make sure that it was not a tumor.

> CT scanning—sometimes called CAT scanning—is a noninvasive medical test that helps physicians diagnose and treat medical conditions.
>
> CT scanning combines special x-ray equipment with sophisticated computers to produce multiple images or pictures of the inside of the body. These cross-sectional images of the area being studied can then be examined on a computer monitor, printed or transferred to a CD.
>
> CT scans of internal organs, bones, soft tissue and blood vessels provide greater clarity and reveal more details than regular x-ray exams. (www.mcrrads.com/pdfs/bodyct.pdf)

The first time we took you to get the scan, you were very scared. You would not let go of my arm and started crying the minute we walked in the room. Then they mentioned an IV and a shot. You started crying even more. We had to reschedule the scan for another day. The next appointment, they were going to give you something to make you drowsy and forget the whole thing.

We did go back about a week later, and this time, we gave you a drug that would help you relax and forget about the whole thing. It was unsettling to watch you go through the process for a scan that took about two seconds. The before and aftereffects of the drugs was what took the most strain on Grandma, Daddy, and me. You did great though. It turned out that you didn't have a tumor on the side of your face after all. Thank goodness!

Dr. Manoukian said that your scan looked great and that he didn't see anything to be worried about. He is still unsure what it really is, but he thinks it might be your sinuses and not draining correctly, or you might be passing a stone and it's having a hard time getting through that area of your face. He recommended that you drink a lot more water. He wants to see you again if your face swells up again. Most stone information is found under the kidneys, but this should give you a little bit of an idea of what a stone is.

What causes kidney stones?

Kidney stones form when a change occurs in the normal balance of water, salts, minerals, and other things in urine. The most common cause is not drinking enough water. Some people are more likely to get kidney stones because of a medical condition, such as gout. They may also be an inherited disease. (healthy.kaiserperma-nente.org/health-wellness/health-encyclopedia/he.kidney-stones.hw204795)

I just hope this part is over. That was enough for me to watch you go through for a very long time. I love you so very much. It hurts me to watch you go through so much pain and I can't help you as much as I would like to. You will always be my baby girl, and I'm going to try my hardest to be the best mom ever.

Love,
Mom

May 22, 2007

Dear Kendall,

Shrek the Third came out in the theater. We went to see it, and it was good. This one is when Shrek's father-in-law, King Harold, falls ill. Shrek is looked at as the heir to the land of Far, Far Away. Not one to give up his beloved swamp, Shrek recruits his friends Donkey and Puss in Boots to install the rebellious Artie as the new king. Princess Fiona, however, rallies a band of royal girlfriends to fend off a coup d'état by the jilted Prince Charming. Princess Fiona is pregnant, and they end up with three babies.

There was a multicultural day at the college this last week. You were dressed in Hawaiian with your little hula grass skirt and a lei. Your class sang two songs. One was "Oh What a Miracle" (♫♪ I'm something special, so very special. There's nobody quite like me ♪♫). The other was about a rainbow. One that I had never heard of before. Everyone was very cute. The funniest part was when you were all introducing your names and who you were representing. Some of the kids could not remember who they were representing, and so they said they were from Lake Tahoe.

I took you and Kasi for a bike ride a couple of weekends. We went to the meadow by Grandma's house and behind Meeks and Taco Bell. You did well until we got to the corner of Grandma's house. You did something wrong. I heard you crash. I turned around, and your nose was bleeding. You hit yourself in the nose with your handlebars. The top of your nose was all beat up as well. I had to carry you and Kasi back to the house and left the bikes on the side of the road. You were okay, but your nose was a little beat up.

We went to Gardnerville for a practice performance with the other kids to prepare for the big night. Your dance performance is scheduled for June 5, 6, and 7 at MontBleu Resort and Spa. You are doing so well in your class. You liked watching all the dancers.

Soccer sign-ups were this week. We signed you up for U-5. I think Daddy is going to be the coach, and I'm going to assist. I think this will be a fun soccer season. I'm actually looking forward to it.

I took you to the dentist for the first time. The hygenist took the little electric drill and cleaned your teeth. She said that it would feel like your teeth were being tickled. You had x-rays taken of your teeth. You did so well. The hygenist said that you were her best patient as a first timer.

You got your kindergarten shots. You got two in one arm and two in the other. Your arm swelled up on one side though. You had a reaction to one of them. You did good though. I am so very proud of you.

Love,
Mom

June 26, 2007

Dear girls,

This is a letter specifically on what is currently happening to our town. This is the most devastating disaster to this community. I am giving you a general letter about the disaster.

Lake Tahoe Fire Destroys 200-Plus Buildings, Clouds Lake with Ash

June 26, 2007

Meyers, Calif.—A raging wildfire near Lake Tahoe on Monday forced hundreds of residents to flee towering flames that destroyed more than 200 buildings, turned the sky orange and fouled the lake's famously clear waters with falling ash.

Many hotels offered free rooms as families clung to one bit of good news: Despite the destruction, there were no reports of injuries.

"All the memories are gone," said Matt Laster, a legal assistant forced to flee his rented home of five years with his wife, two young children and cat. He showed up at a recreation center looking for clothes and a sleeping bag.

The blaze had scorched more than 2,500 acres—nearly 4 square miles—but by early Monday evening fire officials said the blaze was about 40 percent contained. The U.S. Forest Service expects full containment of the fire by Thursday, said Ken Pimlott, assistant deputy director of the California Department of Forestry and Fire Protection.

The blaze, which authorities believe was caused by some kind of human activity, had scorched almost 2,500 acres—nearly 4 square miles—and was about 5 percent contained. However, with the level of containment authorities said the threat against many of the homes had eased.

About 1,000 people had evacuated from the path of the flames, and authorities feared up to 500 other houses could be threatened in this resort area along the California-Nevada state line.

More than 700 firefighters were on hand, but plans to send up airborne tankers and helicopters to drop water and retardant over the heavily wooded, parched terrain were scrapped because of low visibility from the thick smoke.

Firefighters hoped to bring the blaze under control ahead of high winds and low humidity forecast for the middle of the week. Dozens took up defensive positions around South Lake Tahoe High School as flames came within a quarter mile of the 1,500-student school.

"We have a window right now where we're really trying to aggressively attack this fire," said Daniel Berlant, a spokesman for the California Department of Forestry and Fire Protection in Sacramento.

El Dorado County Sheriff's Lt. Kevin House said there were no reports of missing persons, but "the truth is we haven't really been able to get in there and see."

Along the lake's southern shore, a layer of black, mushy ash lapped along boat docks, raising fears the fire also could have disastrous long-term economic consequences for a community heavily dependent on the lake's recreational tourism.

California officials declared a state of emergency, meaning the state would cover all firefighting costs. The National Weather Service issued a dense smoke advisory warning people from South Lake Tahoe to Carson City, Nev., that heavy ash was making it difficult to see and breathe.

The fire began Sunday afternoon on a ridge separating the resort community of South Lake Tahoe from Fallen Leaf Lake, a recreation area where a U.S. Forest Service campground was evacuated.

Firefighters were aided Monday by winds that had slowed to 12 mph after gusting to about 35 mph the day before. Forecasters warned that if high winds and low humidity returned, the fire could threaten more than 500 homes bordering the lake.

By early afternoon Monday, 173 homes had been lost to flames and many others were damaged, along with dozens of outbuildings, authorities said. All that remained of entire neighborhoods in Meyers were the smoldering silhouettes of stone and concrete chimneys.

In other areas, the fire seemed to randomly skip some homes, but downed power lines, trees and debris made clear that life would not return to normal anytime soon, even for those whose homes were spared.

The burned neighborhoods were a hodgepodge of million-dollar vacation homes, cabins and modest houses strung along the east side of the ridge. At least three members of the local fire department were believed to have lost their homes.

Steve Yingling, sports editor for the *Tahoe Tribune* newspaper, had little hope that his house survived. He was leaving for work Sunday afternoon when he heard the sirens.

"I looked back and saw the huge plume of smoke," he said Monday. "That's when I really started to get scared because I know the danger alert that we've had in this area. Especially this year with the mild winter that we had."

State and federal fire officials had warned of a potentially active wildfire season in the Sierra Nevada following an unusually dry winter. The annual May 1 snow survey found the Tahoe-area snowpack at just 29 percent of normal levels, the lowest since 1988.

Fire restrictions have been in effect in the Tahoe National Forest since June 11. The most common cause of blazes in the area is abandoned campfires, according to the U.S. Forest Service.

Anxious residents barred from returning to the fire-damaged area jammed the lobby of Lake Tahoe Community College in South Lake Tahoe, hoping to get word from authorities on whether their homes were still standing. Some left in tears; others were thankful to have escaped the worst. (www.enn.com/articles/6815-lake-tahoe-fire-de-stroys-200-plus-buildings,-clouds-lake-with-ash)

Our friends Jenny, Ryan, Jacob, and Keiran Feliciano lost their home as well. They were barely able to get their dogs from the house. This is all that was left of their home.

There was a bear found in the Gardner Mountain area. The bear was left in the wild after being treated, for all four paws were severely burned, but not to the point that affected ligaments or tendons. The bear will recover.

There were also dead birds all over the high school campus from the poor air quality.

During all the commotion, a couple of days after the fire erupted, the fire jumped onto the highway, and they evacuated parts of the Tahoe Keys area. This was when panic mode stepped in.

I picked you both up from school, drove home, and started to pack up the necessities: clothes, food, important paperwork, pictures, toys, whatever we felt we could not live without. Kendall was crying and scared. You followed me all around the house, telling me that you did not want the fire to come into our house. Luckily, nothing came our way, but it was very scary for all of us. After a few days, we unpacked the car. We were all having a hard time sleeping, and you were having separation anxiety when we would leave.

We are doing fine now, but many of our friends have lost their homes and everything they owned. I would do anything and everything to save you girls. Mommy and Daddy love you both very much.

I made cookies for us to take to the local fire department as well as the police department. We had both of you say thank you for all their help.

This is one of the many maps of the burned area.

Love,
Mom

July 17, 2007

Dear Kendall,

Once again, we are having a birthday party for you after your birthday. You did have a little party at school with all your class. I brought chocolate chip cookies, and we put a candle and some frosting on one of your cookies. It's hard to believe you are five years old. You start kindergarten in September.

We decided to have a party with both you and Kasi at the same time in August. We are going to have a luau and pool party. Little grass skirts and leis. I think you both are going to have a fun party.

Your grandpa is moving to Lake Tahoe from Oklahoma. He will be arriving mid to late August. He's going to be moving in with Grandma for a while. I told you that the other day, and you said, "I love my grandpa." I'm glad that you and Kasi will be able to have a relationship with him.

You had an incident at school the other day. You and Avery were playing outside in the playground when Avery told you to go pee in the castle out in the play area. It just so happens that you did. Someone told Arthur what you were doing, and you stopped. We could not believe that you would do something like this. We ended up not restricting you, but we had a good talk with you about peer pressure and right from wrong. I hope you don't do something like this again.

I took you and Kasi swimming at the local pool. You, of course, were jumping off the diving board most of the time. You are doing really well in the water. You still have to wear a life jacket in the pool though. You just don't have the swimming thing down enough to swim without it in the deep end.

We tried to take Kasi ice-skating with us. She tried it, but it was too much for her. She didn't like not having control of the way her feet moved. Daddy ended up taking her with him, and we skated for a while. You were just being goofy though. You were on the ice more than on your feet. You wanted to keep going, but my feet were getting tired. You ended up getting a blister on your calf. You love ice-skating.

Snuggle Puppy is a book that we read together. Lately, you and Kasi have been reading this book along with me. You try to say all the words, but at the end, all three of us say, "Oooooh, I LOVE YOU!" And you both give each other a kiss. It really is quite funny and very cute.

Speaking of puppy. July 8, we went to the grocery store to get groceries. There were some kids walking around the parking lot trying to get rid of some puppies they had. We asked to see their mom to ask why. The mother of the puppies, nine of them, was not taking care of them any more, and the family could not keep up with feeding them. She was giving them away for free. We borrowed the puppy to ask Daddy. Needless to say, we brought the puppy home with us.

You decided to name him Paintbrush. He has a little white-tipped tail that looks like it was dipped in paint. He is a black-and-white Rat Terrier. He is about six weeks old and is very cute. You have wanted a little dog for a long time now. Kasi is scared of dogs altogether, and Daddy wanted a dog. He wanted a big dog, but I guess we could compromise. Kasi is getting better with him. She's not quite as scared as she was. You, on the other hand, carried him around like he was a doll for the first week. We kept telling you that he was going to forget how to walk or that he was going to pee in your arms. You are getting a little better, but you are a great little mommy to him. You're actually pretty responsible with him. You take him out to go to the bathroom, and you are even picking up after him once he goes potty. It's become a lot of responsibility, but I think it was the next step in our family.

I love you, baby girl.

Love,
Mom

August 21, 2007

Dear Kendall,

Today was your last day at the Child Development Center before you are off to kindergarten. You start kindergarten on September 4. You graduated from preschool July 20.

During graduation, the class sang a couple of cute little songs.

♫♪ Slippery fish, slippery fish
Swimming in the water
Slippery fish, slippery fish
Gulp, gulp, gulp
Oh no, he's been eaten by a...

Octopus, octopus
Squiggling in the water
Octopus, octopus
Gulp, gulp, gulp
Oh no, he's been eaten by a...

Tuna fish, tuna fish
Splashing in the water
Tuna fish, tuna fish
Gulp, gulp, gulp
Oh no, he's been eaten by a...

Great white shark, great white shark
Lurking in the water
Great white shark, great white shark
Gulp, gulp, gulp
Oh no, he's been eaten by a...

Humungous whale, humungous whale
Spouting in the water
Humungous whale, humungous whale
Gulp, gulp, gulp, burp! ♫♪

Right before you left, you started going through this super
cleaning phase at the Child Development Center. You came home
with prizes almost all the time because you were so helpful in class.

Steamers is a restaurant that we took you to a few times for
their fabulous tacos. They would cook Parmesan cheese on the shells.
They were so good. We drove there one day, and you just happened
to notice that they were closed. It turned out that the cooks had left
food out and did not refrigerate it. The next day, they heated up the
food and served it. Everyone who ate there that day had food poison-
ing. The health department closed them down. I'm not sure when
they are going to reopen, but it looks like they are remodeling.

The Great Gatsby Festival. Return to the 1920s during this living history program that is held annually on the second weekend of
August. You will see actors dressed in period costumes as you roam
through the beautiful Tallac Estate on the shore of Lake Tahoe. One
can enjoy antique automobile displays, croquet demonstrations, raf-
fles, live music, and vendors. As a special treat, there is an afternoon
tea on Sunday, which we did not attend, but we walked by it.

Grandpa moved here! Grandpa just moved here from Oklahoma.
This will be the first time he has lived close to the family. You were
so excited. You even wanted him to sit next to you in the car when
we went somewhere. You usually want Grandma to sit next to you. I
even think that Grandma is starting to get a little jealous of Grandpa
being this close.

We went for a hike up to Fallen Leaf with Grandpa, Jeff, and
Tina. Kendall and Tina were on their own mission part of the time,
and Kasi walked with everyone else. We took Paintbrush with us as
well.

Grandpa arrived here just in time for your birthday party. We
combined your fifth and Kasi's second birthday party this year into
one luau. It was a lot of fun. We had hula skirts, leis, coconut cups,

sunglasses, flip-flops, shovels and pails, sunscreen, a beach ball, a limbo game, your pool was all set up, Hawaiian food and cake. It was really a lot of fun! You had Ella, Emarie, and Devin over to help you celebrate.

A couple of things that you and Kasi have said lately.

You asked Kasi if you could pet her baby. She said, "No, she'll bite you."

You told Kasi no for some reason, and she replied back, "What you mean no?"

I am very proud of you. I love you.

Love,
Mommy

August 26, 2007

Dear girls,

We planned a family trip to Idaho to see Mommy's family. We drove in a car for fourteen hours to get there, but we got there. We borrowed Ella and Mateo's DVD player for the trip. I think you watched four movies on the way there.

We stopped at a hotel on the way up, and you both slept together for the first time by yourselves. It was pretty funny. All the positions the two of you were in. I took a few pictures. You ended up with your foot in Kasi's face at one time.

The first thing we did when we got into town was to eat at Taco Time. This is one of Mommy's favorite places. Mommy's favorite thing to order is the Crisp Meat Burrito. Mmmmm. This is where Grandpa used to take me a lot when I would come and visit. When Grandma and I come to visit the family, we would stop there first thing and eat.

We met with Aunt Arlene and Uncle Mike. Uncle Mike has been in politics for about eighteen years. He was the senator for Idaho. They are related through Grandma, distantly. I'm not even sure what the proper title of your relationship to them would be. I know that Arlene is Grandma's aunt.

You were able to meet your Great-Grandma Helen Rice. This is Grandpa's mommy. Kendall wanted to stay at her house while we went to the store, so you felt pretty comfortable with her for just meeting with her. Grandpa stayed at her house though, and he was there. Kasi played with her in the car mostly. She warmed up to her pretty quickly.

Uncle Rob is Grandpa's youngest brother. He has a son named Tyler.

Tyler, I believe, is your distant cousin. He is mommy's first cousin. It took you about fifteen to thirty minutes to warm up to Tyler and his friend Austen. They are about eight years old. Almost too warmed up. Kendall was trying to kiss on them. You were chasing them around the house.

Tyler, at one point, was carrying Kasi around the house like a little sister. When we were putting you to bed, Kasi wanted to give everyone a kiss and hug good night. She walked up to everyone with kissy lips, and the boys didn't know what to do. I think she made them a little nervous.

We stayed in Uncle Floyd's house on Mertle Beach. This is a great house right along the river. You can look out the windows and see the river towards the backyard. This is Mommy's favorite house. We were unable to see Uncle Floyd and his wife, Gerrie. They went on an Alaskan cruise the same time that we were in Idaho. Uncle Floyd is Grandma's uncle.

We were nervous about letting you both outside by yourselves. One, because the river is close to the house. It is very large and moves quickly. It is so large, it is used as a large port area for cargo ships. The other reason was rattlesnakes. The neighbors warned us that they killed two small snakes out in the driveway the night before while we were there.

Uncle Rob took us out on his boat in the river. Grandpa bought each of you a life jacket to go out on the boat. Kendall went out on the hot dog intertube with Tyler and Austen. You were having a great time. At one point, the hot dog tipped over sideways, and you all fell off. You were scared at first, but then Grandpa and the boys helped you. We started to bring you out of the water. You wanted to go back out on the hot dog. You probably would have stayed out on it all day, but it was getting cold and windy. Your teeth were chattering, and your lips were purple. Kasi got on the hot dog after we parked the boat on the beach. This was your first time on an intertube.

We all went bowling with Uncle Rob, Tyler, and Grandma Helen. After the first game, you and Kasi were bored.

It was so hot up in Idaho. We went to a water park. Kendall's favorite part was the wave pool. You were jumping into the waves instead of going over them. Kasi liked the fountain pool. Water was rushing out of pipes like waterfalls and showers. It was the shallow pool.

Aunt Doris, Glen, and Jane invited us over for dinner one night. They have a pool in their backyard. Corey and Amanda came over to join us. Kendall played in the pool with Amanda. You liked jumping off the diving board. Kasi wanted to try the diving board, but when she walked onto it, she got scared. She said she couldn't go off the diving board because she was too wittle.

In town, there is a roller-skating rink. It's the same one that Grandpa skated at when he was a kid. This was the first time you had ever been on roller skates. You did well. Kendall skated by herself for a little bit.

We had dinner with Aunt Arlene and Uncle Mike. One of their daughters, Cory, and her daughter, Kelsey, met up with us as well.

I took you both to the cemetery where your Great-Grandfather Ray Rice and Great-Uncle Larry are burried. This would be Grandpa's side of the family.

The other cemetery is where your Great-Grandmother Lucille Harvey and your Great-Great-Grandparents Olive Biddison and David Chester are buried. This would be your Grandma's side of the family.

We tried to visit a new park every day that we were there. They have a lot of parks, including a train park that Mommy used to play on when I was little. It's a real locomotive that does not move any more.

We saw a lot of family on this trip. We had a very nice family trip. We had fun, did lots of new things, got along with very minimal fighting, and saw family. It was a great trip. It was a long ride home, sixteen-hour drive, but we made it back in one piece.

Love,
Mom

September 27, 2007

Dear Kendall,

You started kindergarten at the beginning of this month at Sierra House Elementary School! Kasi started preschool today at the Child Development Center at the college! It's amazing how much you have both grown up.

We took you to school and later went to your classroom to see how and what you were doing. You had Ms. Hood for your teacher. This is Krista's sister. Krista was a teacher at the Child Development Center where you were going. Having her in the class I think helped because you knew her.

You didn't cry at all. You stood in line with your class until everyone arrived, and then you all walked to your classroom with your teacher. You did so well. We were very proud of you.

So I asked you about your day when you got home. Sort of like a mini interview.

> Mommy: What was your favorite part of the day?
> Kendall: Coloring. I colored a self-portrait with orange hair.
>
> Mommy: Whom did you play with at recess?
> Kendall: Avery, Katherine, Ella, and Laney. I wore a name tag all day.
>
> Mommy: What did you have for lunch today?
> Kendall: A sandwich. I saved some for Grandma.
>
> Mommy: Whom did you sit with at lunch?
> Kendall: Laney.
>
> Mommy: Is there anyone in your class that you know?
> Kendall: Laney is in my class.

Mommy: Did you read books today?
Kendall: We read a kindergarten book together.

Mommy: What else did you do?
Kendall: We went over the calendar, the month and day.

Mommy: Where do you put your backpack?
Kendall: We have a cubby where we put our backpack and lunch.

Mommy: What else did you do today?
Kendall: Played with blocks and took a short nap.

Mommy: Did you have a good day?
Kendall: Yeah. We went to your back-to-school night.

We went to see what you were working on in class as well as meet your teacher and see the classroom. You showed us where you sat in class and who sat by you. There was even a picture of you on your first day of school.

Mommy was making you lunches to take to school, but I noticed that you would usually bring most of your lunch home and not eaten. You had decided that you wanted a hot lunch instead of bringing your lunch. You wanted to be like your friends at school.

You were playing with Avery at school one day, and somehow, you punched her in the face. When I came to pick you up, Avery was crying when her and her mom walked away, and you wouldn't tell me what had happened. We drove over to their house to find out what had happened. It was an accident after all, and you were both playing, but it was still something that we needed to talk about. We do not hit our friends.

There are about four colored cards in class—blue, green, yellow, and red. Each time you do something bad or don't listen, you go to the next color. The more cards you lose, the more trouble you get into. You are normally quiet, but since you started kindergarten, you talk more in class than you are quiet. You lost two cards in one day and lost part of your recess. Ms. Hood said that she moves you around in the room a lot, but it seems that no matter where she puts you, you talk to someone. You are the most sociable in the class. She said that you are great at group activities. You get things moving because you start most of them going.

You play on the monkey bars and regular bars during recess. You don't play with too many of your friends from the Child Development Center anymore. You play with a little girl named Laney Marsh who Mommy knows prior to school starting. You had a playdate with her about a year ago, and you both became instant friends.

You usually have homework every night. It takes about ten minutes to work on them, but we try to work on a few pages at a time. You are learning how to write your letters. You were able to write your capital letters before you went to school, but now you are writing lowercase letters. These are a little more challenging for you. You are getting letters mixed up: *b*, *d*, *s* (you write backwards), *q*, *p*, and sometimes *g*. You're bringing home these little books that are just of pictures, and you are supposed to make up your own story as you read it. You are learning a lot at school. You even enjoy learning. You ask if you can work on your homework.

You're playing soccer again this season. Mommy and Daddy were your coach. We had seven girls total on the team: Adelei Burrow, Maya Harvey, Kaya James, Lexi Kixmiller, Jerra McLaughlin, Kendall Rangel, and Bella Spina. Our team's name was the Silver Foxes.

Everyone on our team was new to soccer, except you. You were the best one on the team and scored the most goals. We had a great season.

You are taking dance class again. You are taking ballet with Ms. Kelly. You really want to take tap dancing, but she said that you had to take two years of ballet first. You are doing more on the bars. You had a walkathon at school. This was an event at your school that was to help raise money for extra programs at your school. We walked around the neighborhood and asked our neighbors for donations to help. You raised over $160. I didn't make it to the event, but Daddy did. You had a lot of fun. You walked forty-seven laps. After the event, we walked around the neighborhood and handed out thank you cards to all the people who helped with their donations. Ms.

Hood's class was the Under the Sea team. You and Avery were doing the laps together for part of the time. Everyone came home in a T-shirt.

Love,
Mom

October 31, 2007

Dear girls,

Happy Halloween! We went down to Apple Hill in Placerville, California, to get pumpkins and to walk around the area for some Halloween spirit. You brought your friend Maya with us too. We picked out our pumpkins and grabbed some apples to take home first so that we could take our time doing other things.

There was a man making balloon animals. You each wanted one, of course, and so he made Kendall and Maya each a dog that swallowed a pumpkin. There really was a little balloon pumpkin in the belly of the dogs that he made. It was cool. Kasi had a pink flower made for her.

Next was the pony ride. I don't know who was more excited out of all three of you girls. I was surprised that Kasi went on a pony, considering that horses usually scare her if we get too close. You picked out the horse that you wanted, and you got it. Kasi followed the lady helping and just let her pick her up and put her on the littlest pony. You all had so much fun. I think you all talked about that more than anything.

You all wanted Kettle Corn, and so we bought a bag. We ate it while we walked around looking at all the crafts and entertainment. We even bought a magnet with four peanuts on it and had the craft person write our names on it. I keep telling you both when we go somewhere that we are going to the nuthouse, referring to home, and so I bought four peanuts referring to the nuthouse. We are officially a nuthouse family.

For dinner, we took you all to the Apple Café. We picked fall-colored leaves that had fallen from the trees before we walked in. Paintbrush went with us too. He loved playing around in the leaves and jumping on them.

We had an eventful weekend packed with fun Halloween things to do. The Child Development Center was having a Harvest Festival.

They had games, cookie decorating, and other fun activities. Kasi was a giraffe, and you were Pegasus.

There was a Halloween carnival at St. Theresa's Church just down the street from our house. Grandpa went with us. He dressed up as a doctor. We went through the haunted house, and it was a little too scary for the both of you. Kasi came out crying, and you were clinging onto me through the whole thing. It was done pretty good.

Sierra House had a fall festival. There were so many games and things to do. There was a Fear Factor table set up with fake blood to drink (Kool-Aid), pumpkin slime for guts to feel, chocolate-covered spiders (chocolate-covered nuts), worms to feel, brains to eat (Jell-O mold of brains), and a couple of other items. You were chosen to eat brains. You ate it too. You were a little grossed out though.

There was a fishing game, beanbag toss, basketball hoops, knock over a duck with beanbags, and a costume contest. You both won the costume contest. You both received a prize for winning.

This year, you carved your own pumpkin. Tried. It was a little tough for you, but you did well for what you carved.

There was a Zombie Walk from Embassy Suites to Tahoe Bowl. This is a few miles' walk. We followed them a couple of times. You were both scared. It was a group of people that were dressed like they were dying. They were all in costume with fake blood all over them. We watched them walk by, and then we went to get Grandma and went back again. On the way to Grandma's, I was trying to get you both to say that you saw dead people in a creepy voice, but you wouldn't do it.

Kahle had a Halloween carnival as well. There were games, an egg hunter in the dark with flashlights, a bounce house, trick-or-treating in the different rooms, and pictures. You mainly wanted to play in the bounce house.

Treat Street is a hotel where local businesses rent out rooms and hand candy out to children as they walk by the rooms. This is one of the safest ways to trick-or-treat. For the past two years, your friend Ross and his family have handed out candy there. Overall, I think we had a great Halloween this year. There were a lot more things going on.

At your school, the teacher, Ms. Hood, assigns jobs to the kids in the class every week. This month, you were the line leader. You oversaw standing at the front of the line and leading the kids in and outside or whenever you left the room. You were told to tell the kids, "Lips and hips and we're ready to go." You put your finger on your lips and your other arm on your hips. You were so proud of this job. You really liked being the line leader.

Happy Halloween. I love you.

Love,
Mom

November 26, 2007

Dear Kendall,

Sierra House had a fall festival at the beginning of this month. None of the family could make it, but you had a good time. You were able to do crafts, games, and face painting.

You auditioned for a part in a play, *Cinderella*, which was performing at one of our schools. Everyone, from kindergarten through high school, could audition for a part in the play. You, unfortunately, did not get the part, but we did go see the play.

At the Bijou Community Park, they had a day of fun set up for all the community. You and Daddy both entered a race to win a turkey or a pie. You ran the girls aged five, twenty-five-yard race. You came in fifth place. You were behind this girl in front of you. Daddy ran the men's 17 and Over 2.7-mile race.

Daddy came in tenth place. He would have placed sixth, but he decided to run an extra lap by accident. He was supposed to run three laps, and he ran four. Neither of you won the race, but you had fun participating. The results were in the local newspaper.

Thanksgiving was delayed for a day. Grandpa had to work on Thanksgiving Day, and so we celebrated it the day after so that we could all be together. We had turkey and all the fixings at Grandma and Grandpa's house. We all played Pictionary after dinner.

You brought home your first report card. You are doing very well in school. You still need to work on your letter sounds and writing your name with lowercase letters. The teacher, Ms. Hood, really enjoys you in her class. I am very proud of you. You are growing so quickly.

You can count and write to 100.

You are coming home with these little books that started off with just pictures and slowly have been small three-to-five-word sentences. Part of your homework is to read your books to someone at home. You have been doing so well with this. You've been reading books with "I see..." and "I like..." You are doing so well. In fact, we went to the local library to borrow books, and I found a book that had these little sentences in it. I had not even read the book with you yet, and you opened the pages and just started reading the sentences all by yourself. You read most of the book. I couldn't believe it.

You've been practicing your letter sounds at school. "A [sound a] apple." "B [sound b] bear." "C [sound c] cat." You've been coming home saying them aloud just around the house.

You can draw hearts and stars all by yourself now.

You can tie your shoes all by yourself. You were getting frustrated when you first tried at school because other kids in your class were able to and you couldn't. One of the little boys in your class taught you how to tie. It was such an achievement when you finally figured it out. Now you want to tie everything by yourself.

I love you, baby girl.

Love,
Mom

December 30, 2007

Dear Kendall,

We had a very busy month in December. I wanted to take you and Kasi out to holiday events throughout the month and see Santa, which we saw a lot this year.

We started by decorating our Christmas tree. You and Kasi both put the ornaments all over the tree. I had to move only a few around this year. Usually, you both put them in one spot on the tree.

At the Heavenly Village, they have an annual event with Santa and characters around the village. We started with sitting on Santa's lap and letting him know what you wanted for Christmas. You wanted an electric Harley scooter again this year, but I told you not to ask for that because you had to be nine years old to have one of those. You asked him for a Christmas Barbie instead. I think that was the first thing you thought of. We decorated cookies. You had your face painted. You had the person paint a reindeer on your face again this year. You went out and showed the person dressed up as a reindeer your face painting, and the reindeer smiled. You had your picture taken with a snowman, gingerbread man, polar bear, and Santa's elves.

You wrote your Christmas letter to Santa, asking for a Christmas Barbie.

There was a Family Craft Night at your school. We walked around the cafeteria to see all the different crafts. You made a snowman ice cream cone ornament, a bracelet, key chain, reindeer antler crown, colored an angel, and made candy cane ornaments.

The Child Development Center, Kasi's school, was having a holiday get-together with Santa and crafts as well. You made trees and snowmen. You were able to see some of your old friends who came to the gathering as well.

Breakfast with Santa at Kahle Community Center. You had your picture taken with Santa. When you sat on his lap, you told him that you wanted a Christmas doll, and Kasi wanted candy. We ate pancakes and drank juice.

We took you both to see a dance performance at Harrah's, which was Marsha's Dance Studio. It was a holiday performance. You and Kasi sat up front, and we sat in the back. There were some good dancers. You both enjoyed it a lot. In fact, you wanted to switch over to Marsha's Dance Studio. I think we are going to finish out the year where you are though.

Your class had a field trip planned this month. Daddy and Grandpa volunteered to help with your field trip. Your class went to Don's Bakery to see the bakery on the inside and to learn how to make a gingerbread house. You were able to decorate gingerbread men and take them home to eat them. You also made a gingerbread house at school. Don asked your class what you were supposed to do after you baked the gingerbread. You raised your hand and said, "Eat them." Everyone laughed.

You were standing in line waiting your turn when Laney, a friend in your class, walked up in line with you. Someone behind you said that she was cutting. You looked at him and said, "No, she's my friend." You stood up for her. I was very proud of you.

I set up with Kahle Community Center to have Santa call our house to ask you and Kasi about confirming that you wanted a Christmas Barbie and Kasi wanted candy. You were so surprised that Santa called our house.

We went to Ernie's Coffee Shop to see another Santa and have cookies. Grandpa came over to watch you as well.

Daddy got a new car for Christmas. The red Isuzu that he had basically quit working. It was having a hard time going up a hill, and the four-wheel drive went out. We needed another car, and this was what he got.

There was a performance at the ice-skating rink, Peanuts on Ice. It was Charlie Brown, Snoopy, Sally, and a few others. The local ice-skating club performed the play on ice. It was cute but very cold in the arena.

This was going to be the first year that Grandpa was here for Christmas with both you and Kasi, but Daddy wanted to spend

Christmas in Los Angeles with all his family too. You both went with Daddy, and I stayed home. You left on December 23 and came back December 29.

You called me from Los Angeles to ask if Santa would come to our house for you. I told you that he dropped your presents off here at your house instead of in Los Angeles. I told you that you could open them when you got back.

You got all kinds of gifts this year. You got a new jacket, a science in a bottle kit, makeup, a zebra pillow, a red blanket, snow clothes, a chalk and dry-erase board, a purple purse, a doll, a Christmas Barbie ornament, a sticker book, and bear handmade by Mom.

You have a new job at school. You were the mat manager. This is where you handed the nap mats out to your classmates for rest time. You oversaw the mats. The assigned jobs that you get at school are rotated throughout the class. It is a big deal to get a job assigned to you. You were so proud.

You were then assigned the lunch count person. Ms. Hood would ask everyone in class if they were hot lunch or cold lunch. After she would add up all the numbers, she would send you down to the cafeteria to let the lunch lady know how many were having hot lunch.

You've had to write your numbers and letters in school lately. You wrote to 100 and counted to 200 all by yourself. I was so proud of you.

You are growing up so fast. I can't believe how much you have grown since you started school.

I am very proud of you.

Love,
Mom

January 31, 2008

Dear Kendall,

At the beginning of January, we were expecting a huge snowstorm. The largest snowstorm in years. Expecting about ten feet of snow at one time. Here is an article from the front page of the newspaper:

Tahoe braces for next storms

January 5, 2008

Up to 44 inches of snow had fallen in some parts of the Sierra Nevada through early this morning, where a blizzard warning was downgraded Friday evening to a winter storm warning, according to the National Weather Service.

Forecasters expected the storm to dump as much as 10 feet of snow on the mountain range by Sunday. Kirkwood Mountain Resort reports getting 60 inches of snow on top of its mountain.

Lake Tahoe was forecast to get between 1 to 2 feet of snow, and the Sierra foothills could get some light accumulation when a third, colder storm moves into the region today.

"It's going to be a mess for travelers," said Chris Smallcomb, a weather service meteorologist. "We expect the road conditions will be hazardous if not impossible."

In South Lake Tahoe, law enforcement were busy last night attending to several spinouts. Telephone services were disrupted in the Tahoe Valley area, as well as cable and Internet outages throughout the South Shore. Sierra Pacific power reports there are no outages in South Lake Tahoe.

City officials spoke this morning on the storm. Currently the city has not determined a need to activate the emergency operating center. Snow crews remains busy and productive, officials said this morning.

Highway 50 is open with chains and/or 4-wheel drive required in some areas.

On Friday night Caltrans closed Interstate 80 across the Sierra, the main east-west link between Northern California and Nevada. This morning, however, eastbound I-80 at Applegate was funneled down to one lane due to snow, according to Caltrans.

The Red Cross set up a 200-bed shelter in Truckee for stranded motorists. (www.tahoe-dailytribune.com/news/update-925-a-m-tahoe-braces-for-next-storm/)

We received about a little over two feet of snow from this storm. Not as big as they thought, but we sure did get hit again a couple more times. We have over 8 feet of snow in some areas of our front yard.

Paintbrush loved it. He was running all over the backyard in the fresh powder. He even made himself a little path around the backyard for himself.

You started basketball a week later because of the storms that came in. We had a lot of snow days from school too.

You started basketball this month. You are such a busy girl. You had five people on your team that you already knew: Kieran Feliciano, Giovanni Fena, Quinn Proctor, Mike Shehadi, and Bella Spina. You just got right in there to get the ball in the rebound, and you made a few baskets. You tend to go straight for the basket to block like you did in soccer at the goal. Your second game, you scored five baskets. You were a superstar! You even take the ball away from other players and block. You are playing well. We are so very proud of you. Even Kasi wanted to join in and play with you. We had to go buy a little basketball for her to practice too. The coaches gave all of you a reversible jersey and a basketball.

You had a playdate with Ella just recently. You and Ella get along very well when it's just the two of you playing together. She was so excited that she was bugging her mom about when you were coming over.

One night in the bathtub, you and Kasi were playing, and you said that you wanted to be Mommy when you grew up. I asked you why, and you said, "Because I love you." It came out of nowhere. It made me smile. I told you that you are so cute, and I love you too. Daddy, on the other hand, was a little nervous about the idea of having two mommies in the house.

You've been in a cleaning frenzy lately. You cleaned your bedroom all by yourself. You were throwing clothes down the stairs and accidentally hit Kasi in the head with a pair of overalls. I asked you what you were doing, and you said that you were cleaning your room. I went upstairs to see, and you really were cleaning up your room. You did very well! I was surprised.

You are becoming more independent. You make your own French toast in the morning. You can make a banana milkshake with a little supervision. Get water or milk out of the refrigerator. You pour cereal for both you and Kasi. You are helping Daddy out in the morning.

We made chocolate play dough over the holiday break.

1 1/4 cups of flour
1/2 cup of cocoa powder
1/2 cup of salt
1/2 tablespoon cream of tartar
1 1/2 tablespoon cooking oil
1 cup of boiling water

Directions:

Mix the flour, cocoa powder, salt, and cream of tartar together in a bowl. Add the cooking oil and the boiling water; (carefully) mix it together well. Cook it over a low heat until it becomes a doughy ball.

Allow it to cool before kneading it well with your hands. Store in an airtight container for 1 to 2 weeks.

Love,
Mom

February 1, 2008

Dear Kendall,

I saw something very sad today in the paper. Remember Heather and Joe Fena? They used to take care of you when you were about a year and a half old, for almost a year. They have a son, Giovanni, who is the same age as you. And Lexington, their daughter, was born on your second birthday, which makes you five. Seth is the youngest of the three kids. He is fourteen months. Heather passed away suddenly on January 27. We're not exactly sure how she died, but they seem to think it was a combination of antidepressants and painkillers. The two drugs mixed and killed her. She was only thirty-three years old. Here is her obituary from the newspaper:

Heather Delaney Fena

July 7, 1974–January 27, 2008

Heather went to join Our Father in Heaven unexpectedly Jan. 27, 2008. She was born July 7, 1974, in Richmond, Calif., a loving mother, she was a 30-year resident of Meyers, Calif.

Heather is survived by her husband, Joe Fena; children, Giovanni, Lexington and Seth; mother and stepfather, Diane and Tom Miller; father and stepmother, Mike Mullinix and Bettike Paul; brother and sister-in-law, Danny Mullinix and Amy Judge; niece, Hailey; nephew, Ethan; and maternal grandfather, Ed Similewicz.

Viewing will take place from 3 to 5 p.m. Friday, Feb. 1 at McFarlane Mortuary and Mass will be celebrated at 2 p.m. Saturday, Feb. 2 at St. Theresa Catholic Church.

Donations for the Fena children may be made at the Al Tahoe Branch of El Dorado Savings in Heather's name. (www.tahoedailytribune.com/news/heather-delaney-fena/)

Grandma and I went to the funeral. Her death hit me hard. I was very depressed for about two days. I don't know if it hit me because we knew her and she was so young, how her kids are going to grow up without their mom, or the fact that I couldn't stop picturing our family in the same situation. I was really scared and upset.

On that note, we saw them a lot with sports. In fact, Giovanni is on your basketball team. We just saw Heather a couple of weeks prior to her death. She had mentioned that we needed to sit down during the next game to get caught up on old news.

I love you so very much.

Love,
Mom

February 27, 2008

Dear Kendall,

Since your whim with chores and cleaning, we have decided to start up a chore chart. We went to the local office supply store and bought you a chore chart. Here are some items that we put on the chart. We have been giving you $1 a week to do your chores. You are allowed to spend your money however you want, but we have given you a few suggestions on how to spend it. You want a two-wheel scooter, and so you have been setting some money aside to save up for it. You have a book fair at school every now and then. You have taken money to buy a book that you wanted. You have bought a pack of gum to stick in your purse. You have been doing very well with your chores. Thank you for helping me around the house.

Daddy took you to the Father-Daughter Dance this year. You were so excited that you were going to the dance. The tickets were sold out last year, and you were not able to attend, but this year, you were able to go. Daddy said that you had a very good time. You came home with a flower and glowed like a ray of sunshine when you talked about the dance to anyone who asked.

Your school celebrated the hundredth day. You have been in school for a hundred days. I volunteered in your class to help with some activities that they had planned for the day. When I arrived, you were in your classroom and glued on a hundred marshmallows to a paper snowman. Then your class moved to another classroom and did another activity. You made a pair of sunglasses in the shape of 100, and you had to stick a hundred stickers on the frame. You made a picture of what you would look like when you turned a hundred years old, and you listened to stories about the hundredth day of school.

For Valentine's Day, you were having a little party in your class at school. You helped me make bracelets for the girls and necklaces for the boys. They all liked them. I went to your class to help with the party and hand out treats. I was even picking on some of your friends in class. I met Isaac. Isaac is a boy in your class that you like. You call him your boyfriend.

You had a week off school for President's Week, and Daddy and I switched to taking days off work to spend time with you. I was going to take you to the gym the day you were with me, but it was not open, and it was too expensive. I found more of a baby gym, Tahoe Tot Spot, down the street and took you there instead. You had so much fun. You jumped on the trampoline into the ball pit and wore yourself out. It's a facility for kids six months to five years. You won't be able to go there very long. You are going to be six years old in a couple of months.

You had a couple of days that you went to friends' houses during your week off as well. One day, you went to Katherine's house. You went with her to get her hair cut. The next day, you went over to Ella's for a playdate. You were so excited to go to their house without Mom. You had a good couple of days.

You have two loose teeth! When you visited the dentist, right before you started kindergarten, he mentioned that you probably would not start losing your teeth until about seven years old. You were so excited to have both bottom middle teeth loose that you called Grandma and Grandpa to tell them. You've been showing everyone, even Uncle Jeff and Auntie Tina when they came over. You can't wait for them to come out. You ask me all the time when they are going to fall out. Grandpa keeps telling you that he's going to pull them out with pliers.

I love you.

Love,
Mom

March 30, 2008

Dear Kendall,

We have been having problems with Motita, our cat, and we ended up giving her away to the SPCA (Society for the Prevention of Cruelty to Animals.) Ever since we got Paintbrush, our dog, she has been peeing and pooping all over the house. Even on our beds. It was becoming so unsanitary that we needed her to go to another family that she would be happier with. She was one of those animals that did not like a lot of attention and did not like to be held. You didn't even notice she was gone for a couple of days, and I finally told you and Kasi that we gave her to another family. I felt bad, but she just wasn't happy in our house.

You started taking the bus after school to the Recreation Center for the after-school program. The first day I picked you up, you were mad at me. You thought that all you were going to do at the Recreation Center was ice-skate, swim, and play. You didn't know that you would have to do some homework as well. I told you that I would find out more about the activities. Later in the week, you went tubing at the Heavenly Ski Resort, ice-skating, and then swimming the next. You were a very busy girl. You really enjoyed yourself though. I can't decide if you're more excited about the bus ride there or the Recreation Center itself.

Daddy and I had a teacher's meeting with Ms. Hood. I was a little nervous to hear what the meeting was going to be about because you had just brought home a red card from school the week before. A red card means that you were not listening and playing in class. The meeting went well. It was a review of your report card. You get along with everyone at school, you do your seatwork when told to do so, but you talk a lot in class. She is okay with this because you don't talk very much any other time. Ms. Hood said that we should be very proud parents because we have a wonderful daughter. That was a huge compliment to us as parents. You are doing so well in class. You are right on top of all the items that you have studied in class.

We were so proud of you! I took you out to dinner to any place you wanted to go as a treat for your good work. We went to Baja Fresh.

We made leprechaun traps for St. Patrick's Day.

What is a leprechaun?

A leprechaun is an Irish "elf." Leprechauns are small, and some say they look like a tiny old man in a top hat and red beard. They are tricky fellows and like to play pranks on unsuspecting people.

Legend says that leprechauns are shoemakers. Curiously enough, they only make one type of shoe. You can tell a leprechaun is near if you hear the tapping of their hammers.

Each leprechaun also has a pot of gold! Some say they bury it in secret places only leprechauns can reach. Others say they hide it at the end of the rainbow. One thing is for sure though. If you catch a leprechaun, he will lead you to his pot of gold and give it to you as a bribe to let them go free.

Here are some tips to putting together a leprechaun trap:

- Since leprechauns like money, you can use coins for bait. If you don't have real ones, use candy coins.
- Rainbows are good to use on or around your trap.
- Color your trap green and decorate it with green items.
- Leprechauns like Lucky Charms cereal.
- Leprechauns are fond of four-leaf clovers.
- A leprechaun will leave a trail of gold and or green glitter, so watch for it!

We made leprechaun traps to try and catch a leprechaun. We did not catch one, but he did leave gold coins in our traps. He even left footprints all over the kitchen table. We covered them with green construction paper. We painted them and put stickers all over them.

On St. Patrick's Day, we made little green derbies and green neckties for you to wear to school. When you went to school, the leprechauns had left a mess in your classroom. They left gold coins in the class for all of you as well.

You lost your first tooth! You have the two middle top teeth and the two middle bottom teeth that are all loose. We were lying in bed when you said that your tooth came out. I looked, and it hadn't.

Two seconds later, you did pull it out. I didn't believe you at first, but you really did pull it out. You looked so cute with a hole in your teeth. You had to look at yourself in the mirror and then called Grandma and Grandpa. You left your tooth in a ceramic tooth holder on your dresser, and the tooth fairy took it. She left you a $1. You were so excited! You were playing in the new hole in your mouth where your tooth used to be.

I found a book at the library called *Loose Tooth*. You were looking at it in the back seat of the car as we were driving to get Kasi from school, and you were reading it all by yourself. You had trouble with conjunction words like *wouldn't* (would not). You read pretty much the whole book by yourself. You like to read. You have a hard time sometimes, and you're not trying, but for the most part, you are doing great.

This month is the hundredth birthday of Dr. Seuss. You read these books a lot.

A new movie came out this week as well, *Horton Hears a Who!* We saw it in the movie theater this weekend.

You had an Easter parade at your school that you needed to make a bonnet for. I made the hats out of paper plates and plastic bowls with a giant coffee filter that I dyed pink and covered them with. I added some ribbon to tie it under your face. We added a pipe cleaner fuzzy flower on top of it. I printed out some spring pictures for you both to color and glue on top of the hats. They turned out so great! Everyone was so impressed. I was even impressed with myself. We went to your school to watch the kindergarten classes parade through the school.

We went to visit Auntie Cindy and Uncle Mike at their ranch house. I love it there. It's always so green and lush. We saw a cow in the early morning that we tried to feed carrots to. He didn't eat them though. We went for a ride on a quad (dirt motorcycle.) I took you and Kasi out on the quad together. You both wanted to go fast and were hollering. We decorated and searched for Easter eggs. I told you that since you were the oldest one, you could only pick up twelve and leave the rest for the younger kids. You counted your twelve, and then you helped Kasi find some. She found twenty-four eggs. She dropped the basket a few times because it was too heavy for her. You got these incredible Easter baskets from the Easter Bunny. We even took Paintbrush with us on the road trip, and he played so long and hard the first day we were there that he slept for almost two days after we got home. He ran from about 7:00 a.m. to about 4:00 p.m. He had nothing but open fields to run in. He was such a happy boy.

Daddy and I took you and Kasi to Circus Circus. This is a large arcade in one of the casinos in Reno. It is set up like a circus. You were even able to see a couple of circus performances. You had your faces painted and played games, won prizes, and had a great time.

Lately, your favorite shows on TV are *Hannah Montana*, *The Suite Life of Zach & Cody*, *That's So Raven*, and *SpongeBob SquarePants*.

Love you,
Mom

April 15, 2008

Dear girls,

The United States is fighting a war over in Iraq and has been for about seven years. One of the soldiers that just died recently was from South Lake Tahoe. He was twenty-five years old and died after a roadside bomb exploded routine patrol in Baghdad.

Hundreds pay tribute to fallen soldier
Body of Army Sgt. Timothy M.
Smith is brought home

April 15, 2008

Hundreds of people lined Highway 50 and Emerald Bay Road near the "Y" on Monday afternoon to honor fallen Army sergeant and South Shore resident Timothy M. Smith as his body was brought home from Iraq.

Red, white and blue signs reading "We will never forget" and "Timmy Smith is a hero" were scattered among the numerous American flags waved by members of the crowd, made up of both those who knew the 25-year-old and those who didn't.

Many of the supporters had tears in their eyes and reached for hugs after the hearse carrying Smith's casket drove slowly past, preceded by members of the Patriot Guard and followed by vehicles from the South Lake Tahoe Police Department, California Highway Patrol, South Lake Tahoe Fire Department and Tahoe Douglas Fire Department.

At one point, the funeral procession stretched from McFarlane Mortuary to the exit of Lake Tahoe Airport, where dozens of supporters had gathered earlier to witness the arrival of Smith's casket.

Although brief applause came from the airport balcony as the plane carrying Smith's body touched down, the crowd soon stood quietly as his casket was carefully unloaded from the plane and placed into a hearse.

The solemn silence of the crowd was broken only by muffled sobs, Monday's howling wind and the haunting cries of Smith's family members as they ran to the plane and wept over Smith's American flag-draped casket.

Smith's body was accompanied on its journey from Iraq by Sgt. Brandon Lords, who was among the soldiers who came to Smith's aid after he was critically injured in a roadside bomb attack in Baghdad on April 7, said Smith's wife, Shayna Richard-Smith.

Lords and Timothy Smith had an agreement that if either one of them was to die overseas; the other soldier would accompany the body of the deceased on its trip home. (www.recordcourier.com/news/2008/apr/15/hundreds-pay-tribute-to-fallen-soldier/)

April 26, 2008

Dear Kendall,

For April Fools' Day, you had not received a homework packet the week before from school. We were trying to get you to tell your teacher, seriously, that the dog ate your homework or to tell Daddy that you peed the bed. You wouldn't say it. Kasi was at school lying down for nap time, and Grandma was rubbing her back. She whispered to Grandma, "Grandma, I peed the bed. April Fools'." Later in the day, she told Grandma, "Grandma, puppy ate my homework. April Fools'." We thought it was so funny that she remembered what we talked about with you that morning, and then she said it in the correct tense and everything. You still didn't say anything.

You've been trying to sound out words and spell them by yourself. You've got a little whiteboard that you write on like you're in class. One day, you wrote, "I love you Mommy and my *gramo* (Grandma) my *holfimuley* (whole family) I love my Kasi and my Daddy." "Mommy, come read my sentence. Oh, it needs a period at the end."

You've been playing on the monkey bars at school a lot lately. You've even got blisters in the middle of your hands from them.

You've been playing Red Rover. Rules of the game: First, split the kids into two teams of equal size. Then have the children line up shoulder to shoulder and hold hands. The two lines should be about fifteen feet apart and facing each other. Decide which team will go first. This team starts the game by choosing a player from the opposing team and adding his name to this little rhyme: "Red Rover, Red Rover, send [insert name] right over."

The chosen child lets go of his teammates and makes a rush for the other line. His goal is to break through the hands of the other team. If he does so, the triumphant child trots back to where he came from with someone from the other team in tow. If he fails, then he's considered caught by the other team and must join it and try to capture his old teammates.

This is where you click the letters that you think are in the word. If you guess a wrong letter, you start to draw a hangman, head, a leg, an arm, etc. For example, I have a word _ _ _ _ _ _. You must guess what it is. Start with the vowels: a, e, i, o, u. The word is w i s h e s.

We signed you up for the last Kids Night Out at the Recreation Center this month. The last time we tried to get you in, it was all booked up. They are usually full before the day even comes. This time, I signed you up about two weeks before the date so that you could get in. You went swimming and had a snack. You were supposed to watch a movie, but we picked you up before they started the movie. You had a lot of fun.

We took Grandpa to Virginia City for his birthday and just walked around. We had ice cream and looked at some of the old buildings. It was a little boring for you, but you still had fun.

You were out of school for spring break, and so we signed you up to attend the recreation center for the whole week. The very first day was a day at Tahoe Gymnastics. You really want to do gymnastics, but it's so expensive. We try to take advantage of it whenever we have the opportunity. You were playing on the bars and hit your mouth on the lower bar. You knocked a tooth out. It was already loose, but it helped to get it out faster. We put your tooth out for the tooth fairy, and she left you two gold dollars. Tuesday, we went ice-skating and bowling. Wednesday, you traveled around the area and ate a variety of different things at different places—Port of Subs, Jalisco's, Rojo's, Sprouts, and a couple of other places. Thursday, you went down to Carson City Swim Center and played in the pool as well as the batting cages. On Friday, you went to the movies and saw Nim's Island. I was going to take a day off from work to spend time with you during your break, but you wanted to go do all these fun things instead. You had a good week. You didn't want to go back to school the following Monday.

Grandma, Daddy, Kasi, you, and I went to Carson City to buy groceries at Costco and decided to take you girls to the Children's Museum. The museum provides exhibits and programs that focus on the arts, sciences, and humanities. Their exhibits and programs are based on Nevada educational standards, current and historical culture, or kinetic movement, and they entertain youth ages two to teen and their families. When we got there, the museum was closing early, so we played for a short period.

Then we went over to the Nevada State Museum to look at a little history of Nevada. You were both scared at first when we went to the mining shaft, but at the end, you both wanted to go again. It's a mock-up of how a mining shaft was built and for what purpose. We try to do a lot of learning and fun activities with you girls, so it seems like we are always doing something.

You had dance rehearsal down in Gardnerville, Nevada, for your show. The whole studio performed from the beginning of the show until the end. You were a bluebird this year. I don't have all the words to the song, but this is like what it was.

♫♪ Bluebird, bluebird, through my window.
Bluebird, bluebird, through my window.
Bluebird, bluebird, through my window.
Oh, Johnny, I'm so tired.

Take a little girl and pat her on the shoulder.
Take a little girl and pat her on the shoulder.
Take a little girl and pat her on the shoulder.
Oh, Johnny, I'm so tired. ♫♪

Your actual performance is May 28 and 29 at MontBleu Resort and Spa.

I love you.

Love,
Mom

May 15, 2008

Dear Kendall,

It was Multicultural Day at Lake Tahoe Community College. Kasi was supposed to perform with her class. They were the first ones up, but she didn't want to do it. She ended up sitting in my lap. Luckily, it was a song that you knew, and you performed it with them. You even said your name and where you were from. I tried to dress you and Kasi in Hawaiian clothes, but she wouldn't even put those on. She gave her costume to Parker instead. I kept you out of school for the day so that you could go and watch the performances for the day.

You both had your names written in Japanese, and each had an origami crane made.

You got up with us for a couple of songs and danced with us. We went with Grandpa as well. Grandpa liked the Middle Eastern dancers as well as you. They were the ones shaking their booty. They did belly dancing.

Other cultures that we saw:

> African tribal drumming—A djembe or jembe is a rope-tuned skin-covered goblet drum played with bare hands, originally from West Africa. According to the Bambara people in Mali, the name of the djembe comes from the saying "Anke djé, anke bé" which translates to "everyone gather together in peace" and defines the drum's purpose. (en.wikipedia.org/wiki/Djembe)

> Aikido demonstration—Aikido, a graceful dance of martial art, offers a unique approach to self-defense and personal development. This article serves as an introduction to the fundamental principles and techniques of Aikido, as well as its rich history and philosophy. (japanwelcomesyou.

com/what-is-aikido-an-introduction-to-the-jap-
anese-martial-art/)

T'ai Chi Chuan demonstration—More
than 300 different known martial arts styles
are practiced in China. There are two Chinese
Martial Art systems, the internal and the external systems. The internal system includes Tai
Chi, Sheng-I and Pa-Qua styles. They emphasize
stability and have limited jumps and kicks. The
external system includes Shao Lin, Long Fist,
Southern Fist, and other styles. They emphasize linear movements, breathing combined with
sound, strength, speed, and hard power impact
contact, jumps, and kicks. (taichifirst.com/tai-
chi-history/taichi-styles.shtml)

Washoe circle dance—The rituals and ceremonies of the Washoe tribe and many other Great
Basin Native Indians included the Bear Dance
and the Sun Dance which first emerged in the
Great Basin, as did the Paiute Ghost Dance. The
Healers of the Washoe tribe used sacred items,
such as eagle feathers and cocoon rattles, to assist
in rituals and ceremonies. Another important ceremony of the Washoe tribe was the Round Dance
and the Pine Nut dance which were associated
with the harvest pinyon (pine nut) and was performed in supplication for increased food supply
and bringing rain. (www.warpaths2peacepipes.
com/indian-tribes/washoe-tribe.htm)

Daddy and I also performed. We danced a couple songs of
Merengue.

Merengue, couple dance originating in the
Dominican Republic and Haiti, strongly influ-
enced by Venezuelan and Afro-Cuban musi-

173

cal practices and by dances throughout Latin America. Originally, and still, a rural folk dance and later a ballroom dance, the merengue is at its freest away from the ballroom. (www.britannica.com/art/merengue)

Filipino songs—a friend of yours from the preschool you used to go to, her mom, Joanie San Agustin, sang two traditional Filipino songs.

Middle Eastern dancing—What is Belly Dance? Raqs Sharqi (pronounced Roks Sharkee) literally translated means "dance from the East." It is the classical and popular folk dance of Egypt and is an integral part of the Middle Eastern culture. (katerinabellydancer.co.uk)

Ballet Folkorico—Ballet Folkorico is a Mexican folkloric ensemble in Mexico City. For five decades, it has presented dances in costumes reflecting the traditional culture of Mexico. The ensemble has appeared under the name *Ballet Folklórico de México de Amalia Hernández*. (en.wikipedia.org/wiki/Ballet_Folklorico_de_Mexico)

Polynesian dancing—Polynesian dance is a group of dance styles including Tongan, Hawaiian style dances such as the Hula, Tahitian, Samoan, New Zealand (Maori) and Fijian. Many of these dances expressed feelings or told stories and were often paired with traditional instruments and storytelling. (danceparent101.com/what-is-polynesian-dance/)

Flamenco, form of song, dance, and instrumental (mostly guitar) music commonly associated with the Andalusian Roma (Gypsies) of southern Spain. (There, the Roma people are called Gitanos.) The roots of flamenco, though somewhat mysterious, seem to lie in the Roma migration from Rajasthan (in northwest India) to Spain between the 9th and 14th centuries. These migrants brought with them musical instruments, such as tambourines, bells, and wooden castanets, and an extensive repertoire of songs and dances. In Spain they encountered the rich cultures of the Sephardic Jews and the Moors. Their centuries-long cultural intermingling produced the unique art form known as flamenco. (www.britannica.com/art/flamenco)

There was also a fashion show at the end. You both had a lot of fun, but it seemed like a long day. We were there almost all day. We could always learn a little more about other cultures and people. That is the neat thing about people being different. You can learn about so many other things from other people's cultures and lifestyles.

I love you very much.

Love,
Mom

May 30, 2008

Dear Kendall,

We took you and Kasi to see this ensemble of musicians and dancers from Ghana, West Africa. You really liked the music, and you were both dancing.

Tahoe Arts Project, with support from Robert and Patricia Dodds, will bring the Kusun Ensemble to Lake Tahoe Community College's Duke Theater at 7:00 p.m. May 2.

The Kusun Ensemble is a group of musicians and dancers based in Ghana. Founded by Nii Tettey Tetteh, the ensemble includes past members of the National Ballet and the Pan-African Orchestra. Although rooted in traditional music, the group has developed a new brand of music and dance that it has dubbed "Nokoko."

The group has created innovative rhythms and dances by fusing bass and lead guitar with traditional Ghanaian instruments to produce a blend of jazz and African music. The ensemble has been entertaining audience in Ghana and around the world.

We also went to see Jenny, Jacob, and Kieran perform their dance numbers. They are in a couple of hip-hop classes with Mrs. Marsha.

We were trying to think of a punishment for you for when you get in trouble. Something that would make you understand we mean business when you do something bad or wrong. We were sitting down talking about it in front of you when Daddy was being a stinker. You told him that we were going to ground him from the TV and from running for eight weeks. He said no because he needs to be able to exercise. You said, "No, Daddy, this is serious. We must take something away from you that will hurt you." You understood what we were trying to do, and you turned it around on him. We were laughing so hard.

The school district is trying to get families to sign up for their kindergartner, and they made this poster. It's for Ms. Hood's class, and you are in it. This means that your mug shot is plastered all over town.

We signed up for soccer again. Mommy is going to try and coach you this year.

You were one of the kids chosen from Ms. Hood's class to receive the Golden Star Student Award. This award is honored to students who do well in class. There are only two students per class that are acknowledged with this honor. We are taking you to the county fair.

You lost another tooth! Now you have your two bottom middle teeth and one top middle tooth missing. So you have three teeth missing in the front. You look funny. Daddy calls you *ventanitas*, "little windows."

Your Daddy and I just celebrated our eight-year wedding anniversary together this month. I cannot believe it has been that long.

You had your dance pictures taken, and you all looked so cute, Little Bluebirds. You had your dance performance at MontBleu. You did very well, other than not looking at the audience during the performance. You would either watch one of the other girls or stare off to the side of the room.

You received an award called the Governor's Challenge. Any student actively enrolled in an accredited California school in grades k-12, or any California teacher may participate in the Governor's Challenge Competition by taking the Governor's Challenge on behalf of his or her school. All students and teachers completing the Governor's Challenge will qualify for a Governor's Council patch and Certificate of Completion. Students and teachers can earn one patch and one certificate per academic year.

To successfully complete the Governor's Challenge, students must be active thirty to sixty minutes a day at least three days a week for a month in addition to the physical activity they engage in as part of their school's regularly scheduled physical education classes. For the purposes of this competition, physical activity is broadly defined and can include all forms of physical activity including, but not limited to, such things as playing basketball, biking, boarding, diving, hiking, lacrosse, soccer, surfing, swimming, volleyball, walking, and wrestling.

You really are good at just about any sport that you try. You like to be challenged though. You also like to challenge Mom as well. I still love you though.

I really like taking you girls to the beach closer to sunset in the summertime. It's not cold, and you don't get sunburned. You were both picking us little shells and playing in the water. Sunsets are beautiful in Lake Tahoe.

We've had this little car for a couple of years now, and you love to drive it. We got you girls a new battery for it at Christmastime, and you've now just had the opportunity to use it. It goes a lot faster than it used to. Kasi was driving around in the street, listening to music in the little car. She drove down the street and picked you up.

Love,
Mom

June 23, 2008

Dear Kendall,

You are officially six years old! You're already saying, "I'm almost seven years old." You just had your sixth birthday at the beginning of this month. I keep telling you not to rush it.

We didn't really celebrate your birthday by throwing you a party this year. We just did a little something for you at school with your class. We sang happy birthday to you and shared little chocolate cupcakes.

For your birthday, Mommy, Daddy, Grandpa, Grandma, and Kasi got you a two-wheel scooter and some roller skates. We thought you would never put the scooter down the moment you saw it, but you were so excited about the roller skates that you didn't even touch the scooter until the next day. You were glad to have both. Grandma even bought you some kneepads, elbow pads, and gloves. Kasi was very disappointed that she couldn't skate with you. We ended up buying her a pair of roller skates as well. You were getting better on them by the end of the day. You are just a sport fanatic.

We went fishing for the Fishing Derby that they have every year in Tahoe. We had a good day too. Kasi won a fishing pole. Daddy and Mommy each caught a fish, and you helped wheel them in. Mommy had to hold the fish to get the hooks out of their mouths. All the blood that the hook was causing from being stuck in his mouth grossed everyone else out.

We took you and sissy to the county fair. You girls had another fun-filled day. You went on rides and pet farm animals—pigs, goats, cows, chickens, rabbits, and even a white turkey. Kasi didn't want to pet any of the animals.

You had a kindergarten graduation. The kindergarten classes all sang a song together in front of all the parents.

♫♪ Start spreading the news
We're leaving today

We want to be a part of it, first grade, first grade
We're ready to go
We've worked very hard
We're going to be a part of it, first grade, first grade
We know our A, B, Cs and our 1, 2, 3s so well
We've worked out sounding out words
And stories to tell
Just ask us to rhyme
We'll say fence and pence
We've learned to share and get along with all our friends
So now we've made it there
We'll make it anywhere
We're on our way
First grade, first grade ♫♪

Mommy took a week off work to spend time with you and Kasi since school was out. Not to mention save us some money.

We went to the Tahoe Paradise Duck Races. The South Lake Tahoe Optimist Club's "A Day in Paradise" duck races and barbecue. We bought a ticket for a duck. They were the little rubber ducks, and each one had a number it. The first-place duck won $500. We didn't win, but we watched them swim down the creek. You even used your duck callers to push them down.

There were activities for you girls to play like games with prizes, a jumping castle, and face painting. You both got these great butterfly paintings on your faces. We had hot dogs in the park as well as the duck races. None of our ducks won though.

There was a block party from the Heavenly Gondola area to MontBleu Resort and Spa. There was Freestyle Moto-X Rock Show, Miss Hawaiian Tropic Northern Nevada State Finals (swimsuit competition), live music on three stages, Flying Elvi skydive team, street performers, Harley/Hot Rod displays food vendors representing some of Tahoe's finest restaurants, art show, craft fair, recreation expo, complimentary bike valet, bounce house, and climbing wall.

Your favorite parts were the Freestyle Moto-X Rock Show and the climbing wall. You climbed the wall twice by yourself. You did awesome too!

We played tennis, went swimming, got ice cream, went on a few bike rides, and went on a small hike with the dogs.

We went to the beach and just played in the sand. You were both trying to bury your legs.

We went to Devin's birthday party, and she had a pony for everyone to take turns riding.

I did say dogs. We were going to puppy sit Stacia's Chihuahua, but it turned out staying at our house, and we adopted him. His name was Chewy, but we changed his name to Chili instead. He is a very cute doggy. You and Kasi can both carry him around and love him. You both fight over whose turn it is to hold him. We must set a timer for you both to take turns holding him. Paintbrush likes him too. They play and wrestle all day long. That is if you girls let him down long enough for them to play. He's adapted very well to our family.

We went to the dentist as well. The dentist said that your teeth looked great, but that they wanted to put a coating over your back teeth to prevent cavities in the future. You walked into the office like no big deal and just sat in the chair, let them take x-rays of your teeth and everything. I even got a picture of you with the fluoride pieces in your mouth. Not one cavity. Great job!

I love you.

Love,
Mom

July 25, 2008

Dear Kendall,

You have had an incredible summer!

You did spend the first week with Daddy. You went on a bike ride, swimming, and rode your scooter. One day, Daddy had you ride your scooter from our house to the Tahoe Keys pool. That was too far for you, five miles. Not to mention swimming and playing tennis once you got there. You were so tired that he had to carry you halfway home. I think it would have been no problem on your bike, but not your scooter.

You are going to the Recreation Center every day since school is out. Here is an idea of the things that you've been doing.

July

Monday	Tuesday	Wednesday	Thursday	Friday
7 Gymnastics Swimming	8 Climbing wall Gymnastics	9 Sacramento Trampoline	10 Ice-skating Bowling	11 Movie Swimming
14 Storytelling at the campground Swimming Ice-skating	15 Arts and crafts at the campground	16 Beach BBQ in Truckee Day Camp	17 Map game Swimming Bike hike Bike day	18 Movie Swimming
21 Mystery Game Swimming Ice-skating	22 Capture the flag Climbing wall Water Slide	23 Disc golf Bike hike Bike day	24 Monarchs basketball in Sacramento	25 Movie Swimming

28	29	30	31	
Walk the plank Swimming Ice-skating	Beach	Sand Harbor Shakespeare play	Pope Beach BBQ	

Your favorite things to do were gymnastics, ice-skating, swimming, and bowling. You didn't get to do the barbecue in Truckee, day camping, or the bike hike the next day because you were very sick.

On the day that you went to Sacramento to see the Monarchs Basketball game, you were stuck in traffic on the way home because of a car accident. Two other cars had collided with each other, and so traffic was not moving in either direction. You sat on the bus for 4.5 hours. You didn't even make it back until almost 8:00 p.m. That was a twelve-hour day for you. You were so exhausted. I'm just glad that you were all okay.

I came to pick you up from the Rec. Center one day and had noticed your eyebrow had been cut and that you were missing a lot of hair. You had lied and said that Halle, a girl that you hang out with at the Rec. Center and from school, had cut your hair with scissors. Her mom yelled at me about Halle's hair. Apparently, you had cut her hair as well as your own. I didn't know this until we got home and talked about it. You wrote Halle a note that said, "I'm sorry for cutting your hair." We made you pay $10 for her haircut. You paid for your haircut as well to fix yours. You had to write, "Lying hurts people" on five pages, top to bottom. You cleaned up dog poop in the backyard and cleaned your room. Daddy and I were not happy with your actions and most of all for lying.

Melissa cut your hair just like hers. The length was to your shoulders in the front and short in the back. Daddy was calling you little Melissa. It does look cute on you.

Your friend Maya stayed the night at our house one night over the weekend. The next morning, the two of you and Kasi had a lemonade stand. We set out on Sierra Boulevard right next to the church up the street from us. You each poured the lemonade and counted the money. You each made $9. We had you split it into three groups—spend, save, and donate. With the money that you were able to spend, we took you to the movies, and you bought snacks with it. We are probably going to donate the money for donation to the Women's Center or perhaps the wildlife place in town.

Daddy had a birthday this month. We didn't tell him happy birthday until late in the day, and he felt bad. He thought we had forgotten about his birthday. We made it up to him though.

You told me the other day that you didn't want to go to the Rec. Center. I asked you why not. You said that you cried and missed me. That was so sweet of you to say. I think you had a rough day too. You really like going to the Rec. Center though. Some of the bigger kids can be pushy though and tend to forget that there are some little people around.

I sure do love you very much.

Love,
Mom

August 14, 2008

Dear Kendall,

We went to the St. Theresa's Country Fair. It was a fundraiser mostly. Admission was one can of food for the charity drive. There were bouncy slides, face painting, games, and performers. You and Kasi ended up going down the bouncy slides the most. There were dance performances from one of the dance studios here in town. We were there most of the day, and so by afternoon, everyone was getting tired and cranky.

We went to the Relay for Life event. It's a fundraiser to help find cures for cancer. There is a part where we take the dogs and walk them around the track as part of the fundraiser, but we ended up not staying lot. Besides, Chili tried to attack all the bigger dogs that would walk by him.

We went to the Wildlife Care facility and saw wild animals and bears that were being taken care of. You got to hold a squirrel.

Kasi had graduation at her school. She didn't graduate, but the kids in her class moving up to kindergarten did. She sang three songs, and she did great!

Your Daddy eats some interesting things sometimes, vegetables with yeast or oat bran on it. It usually looks disgusting but healthy. You've been noticing. You asked me one night at dinner if what you were eating was healthy, and I said yes. You said, "I like it then." That was unexpected, being that you are only six years old and asking that question and knowing what you were talking about.

Since lying has been as issue with you, we want to make sure that you understand that lying is not a good thing. We've been trying different ways to teach you about lying. I asked you one night if Daddy had put sunscreen on you before you went to the Recreation Center. At first you said no, but then you changed your mind and said that he did, and you just forgot. I think you are starting to understand what lying means. I was very pleased with you and told you that I was proud of you for telling the truth.

You had a tooth that was loose. You were pulling on it, and it just was not ready to come out all the way. We were eating pizza, and suddenly, it was gone. I asked you where it went, and you didn't know. You ended up swallowing it. You were so bummed. You didn't think the tooth fairy would come, but she did.

We had another bed given to us, but it is a big bed. Now both you and Kasi have a queen-size bed in your room. You've been sad though. You like having your own bed, but I think you get lonely in that big bed all by yourself. You always ask Kasi if she wants to sleep with you. It helps keep you both apart and wanting to play as much before bedtime.

You went to Los Angeles with Kasi and Daddy to see your cousins and Abuelita. You both had a good time seeing your family. You played with Diego and Marianna a lot. You were so excited to go. You kept asking when you were leaving. The day after you got there, Daddy took you to the emergency room. You were vomiting and had a fever. It turned out that you had a kidney infection. They put you on medication, and by the end of the day, you were feeling better. The doctor also mentioned that you had protein in your urine. He wanted us to make a follow-up appointment for you when you got back.

You were playing at Grandma's house with the cell phone. She asked you who you were calling. You said, "No one. I'm texting my boyfriend." This is the new fad right now. Everyone has a cell phone and texts.

August

Monday	Tuesday	Wednesday	Thursday	Friday
				1 Soccer clinic
4 Swimming Soccer Clinic	5	6 Wild Island	7 Soccer clinic Bowling	8

11	12	13	14	15
Fat Burgers Gondola Swimming	Trolley to camp Richardson Ice cream Beach	Meeks Bay Beach	Tahoe Queen	Arcade Swimming
18 Bike to mini golf Swimming	19 Bike to lunch Climbing wall Snow cones	20 Ice-skating Carnival days	21 Swimming	22
25 You didn't go all this week	26	27	28	29

I love you very much.

Love,
Mom

September 27, 2008

Dear Kendall,

You started second grade this month. We were so excited for you. You are in a first and second grade combo class. Ms. Hood is your teacher again. You were hand chosen to be in this class. The children were hand chosen. They had to have maturity and smarts to handle a harder class. First graders are still learning first-grade work, and second graders are learning second-grade work. There is a time in class that you are working on the same things together though.

Ms. Hood said that you are doing very well in this class. She said that you finish your seatwork quickly, and then you move over to help a second grader with their work, and you can help them.

Kids in your class: Adelei Burrow, Caleb Caramazza, Maya Harvey, Jacob Hasslinger, Nathan Hayward, Taylor Luecke, Colby Lyle, Mitza Marmolejo, Jerra McLaughlin, Jordan Ruvalcaba, Alan Storie, Dominic Thoma, Paolo Torres, Lexy Trejo, Pedro Vargas, Juan Vazquez Valdez, Justice Weimer, and Erynn Wilson. Adelei Burrow, Maya Harvey, and Jerra McLaughlin were all your soccer team. Nathan Hayward, Mitza Marmolejo, and Dominic Thoma were all in your class last year.

You are taking the same bus as last year after school to the Recreation Center and taking the same bus, 31. Judy is your bus driver. You really like Judy.

You had your first math test at school. It was a timed three-minute addition test, and you scored 100 percent on it. You really like math.

You had a back-to-school night at school. You were not supposed to go, so you stayed home with Grandma. I talked to Ms. Hood about you being in her class this year. She was glad to say that she had chosen you for this class and that you are doing extremely well in this class. She said that she was very proud of you. You are opening up more in class this year as well. She mentioned that you get along with everyone in the class, and when it's time to do seatwork, you are usually the first one to get started and usually the first one to finish. You really like your class. You have a lot of friends in your class.

You had your walkathon. This year, Daddy and I were both there to participate. You are so lucky to have both of your parents involved in your life and education. We both love you very much. You raised $240 and walked forty laps. We are so proud of you. After the fundraiser, we made thank you cards to the people who donated money to let them know that we appreciated their donation and to let them know how many laps you walked. You even said thank you to all of them.

Sometimes we lay out clothes for the next day so that you are not struggling with it in the morning. You picked out a shirt, black, that did not go with a pair of pants that did not match. I told you that they didn't match, but you said, "Daddy said that black goes with everything." I just laughed and didn't know what to say.

You came home with a schoolyard rhyme that made me laugh, and I just had to write it down. You did all the actions with it and the attitude. It was funny. Not too long after you started singing it at home, Kasi started singing it too.

♪♫ 1, 2, 3, 4
That's the way, ah huh, ah huh, I like it
You go your way; I'll go my way
Peace crunch, captain crunch
Brick wall, waterfall
You think you got it all, but you don't, we do
So, poof with the attitude
Bang, bang, choo choo train
Roll it up and shake that thing ♪♫

Dancing with the Stars is a popular reality show that is on, and you watch a couple of seasons of it, but it's on right at bedtime. There is a guy on the show, Mario Lopez, who you were rooting for one season. You saw him on another show the other day and said, "Mario Lopez. He's just the cutest thing."

Mario Lopez performs with Karina Smirnoff on *Dancing with the Stars*. You were so excited when they came on. You were cheering for them all the way to the end.

You and Kasi made your own dinner. You were excited to make dinner, and it was easy enough for you both to make it. I did all the cutting of the food, but you put it together. We've made it a couple of times since then.

Thursday Night Special—have the kids make their own
From: Oklahoma Church Cookbook

Servings: 1
Prep time: 15 minutes
Cook time: 45 minutes to 1 hour

Ground beef patties (1 patty per person)
1 cup of potatoes (1 small potato)
1 cup of carrots
1 slice of onion per patty (substitute with onion powder)

Directions:

1. Make a meat patty and place it in the center of aluminum foil large enough to wrap the meat and vegetables together.
2. Season the patty with salt and pepper.
3. Place the cups of potatoes and carrots on top of the meat patty.
4. Top it with the onion.
5. Bake, wrapped up at 350°F for 45 minutes to an hour.

You were singing a song in Spanish, "Te quiero tonto asi." I asked you what that meant, and you said, "Talk to the foot." It means "I love you that way."

I sure do love you. You make me laugh so much sometimes.

Love,
Mom

October 31, 2008

Dear Kendall,

Our last soccer game was this month. The team did well. Some of the other coaches complained that we were not playing right, but we still won most of our games. They said that we should have forwards and defensive players designated, but there was nothing mentioned in the rulebooks, so I just let you all run and play whatever position you wanted to. One game, the coach asked us to let their team score just once. I talked to you all and told you to pretend like you were going for the ball and missed it so that they could score. None of you wanted to let them score, but you did anyway. I was so proud of all of you girls, except for one girl, Haley. She didn't come out on the field once, even during practice. We all tried to include her though. I think I'll coach you and Kasi's teams next year. Next year, it will be your last year in U8 and Kasi's first year playing, U4. After U8, the games are more competitive.

We had a pizza party with our team and handed out awards and pictures then. Everyone received a trophy, even Kasi. We had a trophy left over from someone who was supposed to be on our team, but they moved.

We went to the Kokanee Salmon Festival. Each year, the bright red Kokanee salmon return to spawn in their home stream of Taylor Creek. Visitors delight in watching the agile fish as they swim upstream to their home waters. We also saw Sammy the Salmon walking around.

Oktoberfest at Camp Richardson was fun. This is a welcome to the fall event, featuring great food, music, a kid's carnival, and the famous beer and wine garden. German food and desserts, craft booths, live music, pumpkin patch, bouncy castle, face painting, and hayrides. Daddy did the Stein holding contest and won second place. He won a gift certificate for the whole family to go to dinner at The Beacon, a very nice restaurant down by the lake.

We had your school pictures retaken. Your first picture was not very good, and normally, you take a great photo. This time, I stayed home and curled your hair under to wrap a little more around your face. It turned out much better than the first one. You also have three teeth missing in the front.

You went on a field trip with all the first-grade classes. You went to the Corley Ranch. The Corley Ranch is a working ranch for raising cattle, performing horses, and hay. You went through the straw maze, walked around the ranch, saw animals, and picked a pumpkin from the pumpkin patch.

St. Teresa's Catholic Church had a Halloween carnival and haunted house. We try to do this every year. You went in the haunted house with Jordan Malkus, a friend from soccer as well as school. We went through the not so scary version. You were a little scared because you didn't know what to expect, but you did good. Kasi didn't go through with us this year.

The Halloween carnival at Sierra House was fun as well. We arrived kind of late this year, but you came home with a lot of crafts you worked on. We did a few gingerbread ornaments and glass bulbs. You entered the Halloween costume contest this year, but you didn't win. You dressed as a snow princess. You always want to wear a dress for Halloween. We found the costume at Target this year. It was a long dress with long sleeves, and so I was okay with you getting a dress this year. It's normally very cold on Halloween, and so we must dress warmly. Kasi was Scooby-Doo this year.

Happy sixth birthday! We were going to take you both to Disneyland this year instead of throwing you a birthday party, but we didn't have enough money, so we had another Halloween birthday party for you and Kasi. We had it at the bowling alley, and you each invited a few friends. Most of your friends are the ones that showed up though. We made Halloween cupcakes, and everyone blew out a candle on their cupcake. We ate pizza and made a couple of Halloween candy necklaces.

The zombie walk was smaller this year than last year. Kasi didn't want to see the dead people. You got out of the car with me and got closer to see all of them. There were a couple of kids your age this year. We decided that we were going to try and dress up for it next year.

On Halloween night, we went to Treat Street, a hotel rented out by businesses that hand out candy to local kids. It's a safe way to trick-or-treat. Then we went to the Christian Fellowship Church. They had a carnival for families to come and participate in. They had a lot of fun games and candy. We never really went door-to-door trick-or-treating. You both got enough candy to last you for a while.

We had our teacher conference with Ms. Hood this month. She spoke very highly of you. She is so proud of you! This is good, considering that we are proud of you all the time. She said that you are opening up so much more in class this year. You are finishing your seatwork and helping the second graders with their work.

We love you very much. We are very proud of you!

Love,
Mom

November 5, 2008

Barack Obama elected 44th president
"Change has come to America," first African-American leader tells country
By Alex Johnson
Reporter
msnbc.com

Wed., Nov. 5, 2008

Barack Obama, a 47-year-old first-term senator from Illinois, shattered more than 200 years of history Tuesday night by winning election as the first African American president of the United States.

A crowd of nearly a quarter-million jammed Grant Park and the surrounding area in Chicago, where Obama addressed the nation for the first time as its president-elect at midnight ET. Hundreds of thousands more—Mayor Richard Daley said he would not be surprised if a million Chicagoans jammed the streets—watched on a large television screen outside the park.

"If there is anyone out there who doubts that America is a place where anything is possible, who still wonders if the dream of our founders is alive in our time, who still questions the power of our democracy, tonight is your answer," Obama declared.

"Young and old, rich and poor, Democrat and Republican, black, white, Hispanic, Asian, Native American, gay, straight, disabled and not disabled, Americans have sent a message to the world that we have never been just a collection of red states and blue states," he said. "We have been and always will be the United States of America.

"It's been a long time coming, but tonight, because of what we did on this day, in this election, at this defining moment, change has come to America," he said to a long roar.

McCain notes history in the making

Obama congratulated his opponent, Republican Sen. **John McCain** of Arizona, for his "unimaginable" service to the United States, first as a prisoner of war for 5½ years in North Vietnam and then for nearly three decades in Congress.

McCain called Obama to offer his congratulations at 11 p.m. ET, Obama's chief spokesman, Robert Gibbs, told NBC News. Obama thanked McCain for his "class and honor" during the campaign and said he was eager to sit down and talk about how the two of them could work together.

"The American people have spoken, and they have spoken clearly," McCain told supporters in Phoenix, saying that he "recognized the special significance" Obama's victory had for African Americans.

"We both recognize that though we have come a long way from the old injustices that once stained our nation's reputation and denied some Americans the full blessings of American citizenship, the memory of them still have the power to wound," McCain said.

"Let there be no reason for any American to fail to cherish their citizenship in this, the greatest nation on Earth," said McCain, who pledged his support and help for the new president.

President Bush called to congratulate Obama and promise a smooth transition of power on Jan. 20, White House spokeswoman Dana Perino said.

"Mr. President-elect, congratulations to you. What an awesome night for you, your family and your supporters," said Bush, who invited Obama and his family to visit the White House as soon as it was convenient.

The president also called McCain to say that he was proud of the senator's efforts and that he was "sorry it didn't work out."

"You didn't leave anything on the playing field," Bush said.

Broad, deep victory

Campaigning as a technocratic agent of change and not a path breaking civil rights figure, Obama swept to victory over McCain, whose running mate, Alaska Gov. Sarah Palin, was seeking to become the nation's first female vice president.

Obama beat McCain by 52 percent to 46 percent, and he could realistically claim a mandate with nearly two-thirds of the Electoral College. As of Wednesday afternoon, he had 349 electoral votes compared to 173 for McCain, with only North Carolina and Nebraska's 2nd Congressional District left to declare.

And Obama should have a strongly supportive Congress to work with. Not since 1993 has an incoming president had such strong majorities in both houses of Congress.

Democrats will hold 258 of the 435 seats **in the House** and at least 54 of the 100 seats **in the Senate**, where two independents also caucus with the party. Four seats remained undecided, meaning the party mathematically could reach a procedurally important "supermajority" of 60 or more votes in the Senate, but NBC News projected that it would not reach that threshold. (www.nbcnews.com/id/wbna27531033)

November 30, 2008

Dear Kendall,

We are trying to buy a house! Postcards were sent out in the mail for an open house, and we went to see the house. We wanted to know why the price was lower than what the norm was for Tahoe. We thought it was a mobile home or something. It's beautiful inside! It's 1,500 square feet, has three bedrooms, two bathrooms, two-car garage, and it's all new. You said, "If we had a $100, we could live here. I really like this place." I wish that were true.

Kasi's school had a Harvest Festival. We decorated cookies and played some games. You both dressed up in your costumes and saw all your friends dressed up. They held it inside the classroom this year because it was raining outside. It was a little crowded. You both had fun though.

You lost another tooth in the front. We have been giving you a hard time telling you that soon you won't be able to eat because you have no front teeth.

You started having spelling tests. Ms. Hood sends home a list of words that you practice all week with and have a test on the following Friday. You have come home with 100 percent every test so far. I took you out to your favorite restaurant, Orchids-Thai Food, for getting a 100 percent on your test. You got to stay up a little later than Kasi one night. You really are doing very well in school. You also love math. There was an open house at Harrah's arcade for free games being advertised. I decided to take you to the arcade for scoring 100 percent on another spelling test.

You, Daddy, and Kasi all participated in the Turkey Trot this year. The Turkey Trot is an annual race that the Optimist Club puts on every year to help raise donations for Christmas Cheer and the Food Pantry. Kasi placed eighteenth in her race. Daddy placed third in his race and won a pumpkin pie. You were the big winner and won first place in your category and won yourself a turkey. Thanks to you and Daddy, most of Thanksgiving was paid for. During your race, you were ahead, looked around you, and noticed that you were in the lead and then slowed down a little and smiled. You are quick on your feet. We were so proud of you.

GIRLS 3 AND 4—25 YARDS TIME

1.	Addison Castle	6.42 seconds
2.	Jenna Pevenage	6.68 seconds
3.	Mhara Parsh	7.67 seconds
4.	Pitige Linsey	7.97 seconds
5.	Sofia Wagner	8.02 seconds
6.	Kyla Schauben	8.42 seconds
7.	Sydney Bareus	8.56 seconds
8.	Erika Strain	8.74 seconds
9.	Kiana Buchholz	9.02 seconds
10.	Sawyer Villanueva	9.06 seconds
11.	Madison Nelson	9.19 seconds
12.	Olivia Hall	9.84 seconds
13.	Avi Villarreal	9.92 seconds
14.	Vanessa McRoberts	10.13 seconds
15.	Allie Sipe	10.72 seconds
16.	Hailey Tossi	12.43 seconds
17.	Leilah Enterline	12.65 seconds
18.	**Kasi Rangel**	**14.16 seconds**
19.	Taylor Schwindt	16.35 seconds
20.	Simone Sitchon	16.72 seconds
21.	Yona Abiko	19.51 seconds
22.	Ella Mastromatteo	26.56 seconds

GIRLS 6—50 YARDS

1.	**Kendall Rangel**	**9.19 seconds**
2.	Tyler Pevenage	9.27 seconds

3.	Madison Riley	9.55 seconds
4.	Carissa Buchholz	9.69 seconds
5.	Erin Eschleman	9.97 seconds
6.	Bella Spina	10.14 seconds
7.	Eliana Carney	10.27 seconds
8.	Nina Seemann	10.63 seconds

MEN'S 17 AND OVER—2.7 MILES

1.	Doug Cichowicz	19min 46 seconds
2.	Neal Chappell	20min 25 seconds
3.	**Arturo Rangel**	**20min 30 seconds**
4.	Paul Amato	22min 46 seconds
5.	Edward Apodara	25min 13 seconds
6.	Armando Llamas	26min 14 seconds
7.	Refugio Pineda	28min13 seconds
8.	David Gram	10min 41 seconds

Thanksgiving was very good. We went to Grandma and Grandpa's house. We played a few games, watched a movie, and made some crafts. It was a very good day with very moist turkey that you won and a pie that Daddy won.

We were playing UNO, and you had to draw two cards. You told her that she should be ashamed of herself.

You wrote a letter to Santa at school. I asked you to write another one for me to send in the mail for Santa.

Dear Santa, how are you Santa? For Christmas I would like a laptop, Heelys and a necklace for my mommy. Sincerely, love Kendall.

What are Heelys? They're shoes that roll! These one of a kind, powerful, lightweight athletic shoes feature a single, stealth wheel housed

200

in the heel, allowing athletes of all skill levels to walk, run and transition to a roll at any moment. Roll into all situations, or simply remove the wheel and transform your Heely's into a pair of fashionable street shoes! (www.amazon.ca/Heelys/dp/B071ZG1QP3?th=1)

I never wanted to buy these shoes for you. They are dangerous. I love you.

Love,
Mom

December 31, 2008

Dear Kendall,

They had craft night at Sierra House for the holidays this year again. We love doing craft things.

Breakfast with Santa! We went to Kahle and had breakfast with Santa. You told him the same thing you wrote on your letter to him: "For Christmas, I would like a laptop, Heelys, and a necklace for my mommy."

Kasi asked for snow.

This year, you received a phone call and an email from Santa. He called to ask you if your letter was true in what you asked for. The email came from Santa with your picture on it and your name on the Nice List.

Abuelita, Angelica, Israel, Diego, and Mariana came to visit us for Christmas this year. They arrived two days before the snow really hit hard. We got our first snow this month Christmas Eve night, which was about a foot and a half in one day.

Paintbrush did good with them all in our house. He mainly wanted to like Diego and Mariana's faces. Diego was terrified of him. He would scream whenever Paintbrush got close to him.

You all got a lot of presents from Santa this year. You and Kasi each received a laptop computer, a Build-a-Bear kit, slippers, and more. You got a bathrobe. You have been asking for one of these for a while now.

The laptop that you got looks like a real computer, but the screen is more digital. You can either use the mouse on the laptop itself or the mouse on the side. You played with it all Christmas Day. You even have a couple of digital pets that you're taking care of—a dog, cat, and a duck.

The day they all left, you, Kasi, and Daddy all went back with them. You ended up going to Los Angeles to visit the rest of the family for the holidays. You are due to come back after New Year's.

We ended up not getting the house. We could not afford the monthly payments of $1,400 a month. We'll have to try another time.

I love you.

Love,
Mom

December 12, 2008

Dear friends and family,

All I want for Christmas is my two front teeth. This is what Kendall is asking for this Christmas. She's missing three teeth in the front.

Art and I, on the other hand, are singing a new song. This picture is a picture of the new house we are trying to buy this year. This house was advertised in the newspaper, and postcards were sent out to local residents about an open house. We went to the open house to see why it was so cheap for Tahoe. We thought there was a catch, and so we had to see it for ourselves. It is indeed a house. It is a 1,500-square-foot home, three bedrooms, two bathrooms, single story, with a two-car garage just four blocks from the lake. The price is $269,000.

I have lived in this block three times before. We lived in a townhouse across the street. Mom's lot is about four blocks down the street from this house. I think we were meant to live on this street.

Here is a little more information about the house and why we might be able to buy a house in Tahoe. http://www.saintjosephclt.org/.

Kendall has been asking Santa for a laptop, and Kasi has been asking for snow. Kendall has expensive taste. We have not received any snow this year yet. We had one small storm that didn't even leave a mark on the ground. The ski resorts have been making their own snow to open. It's been very slow in town. There are not that many people.

Kendall is doing very well this year in school. She was handpicked to be in a first/second grade combo class. Only kids that had maturity and could handle the challenge of being in a class with second graders were chosen. Her teacher said that she does well in class and that there have been times that Kendall finishes her work in class and will offer to help the second graders with their studies.

She has Art's personality, very energetic and looks like him. She's even built like him physically. She's tall, skinny, and all muscle. She has my stubbornness though. She even got a haircut this summer. It looks short to me.

Kasi is doing very well. She is going to preschool three days a week and with my dad two days a week. She is Grandpa's little precious. She's got him wrapped around her finger. They have grown a bond between the two of them. It's very cute to watch them together.

Kasi is my mini me. She looks just like I did when I was her age. She's the mellower child of the two. She also has my stubbornness as well. Sometimes the two of them together is very challenging. Everyone at school likes her, and she gets along with everyone. She will have two more years of preschool before she starts kindergarten. We can't wait! Childcare is so darn expensive!

Both the girls have their birthdays in the summer, but this year, we had their birthdays around Halloween. We had one party and switched things up a bit. We had a Halloween party at the bowling alley. The kids had fun and ate pizza. Kendall was a snow princess, and Kasi was Scooby-Doo.

We have a Turkey Trot every year at one of our parks. This year, Kasi ran twenty-five yards and placed fourteenth. Kendall ran fifty yards and placed first. Art ran 2.7 miles and placed third. Kendall won a turkey, and Art won a pumpkin pie. So we were pretty set for Thanksgiving this year.

Art has two classes away from his bachelor's degree. He talked to a counselor the other day at the local college and found out that if he takes one more class at the local college as well, he will receive his associate degree as well. He is pretty much getting two degrees at the same time.

He is still working for the college assisting the Hispanic community with classes. He also does a lot of outreach in the community as well as teaching a Foster and Kinship Care class at our Family Resource Center. He is still on the Boys and Girls Club Board and the Gang Task Force Board. He also started a new Hispanic club at the college. As you can see, he is still a very busy man.

He has lost a lot of weight and has become a health fanatic. He has now chosen to be vegetarian, almost a complete vegan. He'll eat a little cheese and eggs every now and then, but not very much. He looks great! He changed his diet after he found out how high his cholesterol was. I wish I had his control and determination.

I am still working at the County of Education. It's Head Start and State Preschool. I am the secretary for fourteen different sites and the only secretary in Tahoe. Our main office is in Placerville, an hour away. I have been here a little over a year now, and it's still a challenge and struggle every day. I work mostly with low-income families.

I am trying to get my act together. I have been going to the gym now for almost two years at six every morning. I haven't lost any weight, but I have gained muscle, which can still be discouraging since muscle weighs more than fat.

I coached Kendall's soccer team this year. This was my second year coaching. Our team kicked butt too. We won almost every game. I will probably coach both Kendall and Kasi's teams next year. This will be the first sport Kasi will play. She basically practiced with us on Kendall's team this year though. She kicks and dribbles better than some of the other kids three years older than her.

We now have two dogs. We thought one was going to be a Rat Terrier, Paintbrush, but he's about five times the size he was supposed to be. And then we have a Chihuahua, Chili. They are inseparable. The little one whines when the big one goes for a run with Art. The girls always fight over who gets to hold the Chihuahua. He is so small and perfect for Kasi. She tries to hold him all the time.

Overall, the economy is horrible in Tahoe, just like everywhere else. There were only three jobs listed in the newspaper today, and more jobs were lost. Luckily, our jobs seem secure right now. We just hope things get better soon. Most of the local small family businesses are disappearing left and right. The cost of housing and gas has gone down dramatically, but the housing prices are still a little high for low-income locals to buy. We hope we get this house that we're applying for. Keep us in your thoughts.

Here are some pictures of things that we have done this summer. Participated in a walkathon at school, beach with Grandma, cruzin' in the car, fishing, county fair with Grandpa, Kasi was a pirate, Kendall did some rock climbing, roller skating, Art won second place in a Stein Holding Contest, and watched a zombie walk for Halloween. We also went on some hikes, rode bicycles, ice-skated, went swimming, played tennis, and much more. We try to stay busy almost every weekend. We had a busy year.

We hope you all had a great year and hope the New Year is better than the last. We love you all.

Love,
Jeanna, Arturo, Kendall, Kasi, Paintbrush, and Chili

January 19, 2009

Dear girls,

Today is Martin Luther King Jr.'s celebrated birthday. Martin Luther King Jr. was a civil rights activist who made the struggle to change conditions in America and to win equal protection under the law for citizens of all races. It may be hard to believe that less than fifty years ago, America had separate drinking fountains for Whites and Blacks and "colored balconies" in movie theaters.

The famous speech delivered in 1963 to more than two hundred thousand civil rights marchers at the Lincoln Memorial in Washington, DC:

> I have a dream that one day every valley shall be exalted, every hill and mountain shall be made low, the rough places will be made plain, and the crooked places will be made straight, and the glory of the Lord shall be revealed, and all flesh shall see it together."
>
> This is our hope. This is the faith that I go back to the South with. With this faith, we will be able to hew out of the mountain of despair a stone of hope. With this faith we will be able to transform the jangling discords of our nation into a beautiful symphony of brotherhood. With this faith we will be able to work together, to pray together, to struggle together, to go to jail together, to stand up for freedom together, knowing that we will be free one day.
>
> This will be the day when all of God's children will be able to sing with new meaning. My country, 'tis of thee, sweet land of liberty, of thee I sing. Land where my fathers died, land of the

pilgrim's pride, from every mountainside, let freedom ring.

And if America is to be a great nation, this must become true. And so let freedom ring from the prodigious hilltops of New Hampshire. Let freedom ring from the mighty mountains of New York. Let freedom ring from the heightening Alleghenies of Pennsylvania. Let freedom ring from the snowcapped Rockies of Colorado. Let freedom ring from the curvaceous slopes of California. But not only that, let freedom ring from Stone Mountain of Georgia. Let freedom ring from Lookout Mountain of Tennessee. Let freedom ring from every hill and molehill of Mississippi. From every mountainside, let freedom ring.

And when this happens, and when we allow freedom ring, when we let it ring from every village and every hamlet, from every state and every city, we will be able to speed up that day when all of God's children, Black men and white men, Jews and Gentiles, Protestants and Catholics, will be able to join hands and sing in the words of the old Negro spiritual:

Free at last. Free at last.

Thank God almighty, we are free at last. (www.npr.org/2010/01/18/122701268/i-have-a-dream-speech-in-its-entirety)

Death came for King on April 4, 1968, on the balcony of the Black-owned Lorraine Hotel just off Beale Street. While standing outside with Jesse Jackson and Ralph Abernathy, King was shot in the neck by a rifle bullet. His death caused a wave of violence in major cities across the country.

King's assassination was international news. Here, London newspaper headlines about his death. April 7, 1968.

January 20, 2009

Dear girls,

Today was the day for the Forty-Fourth Presidential Inauguration.

My fellow citizens:

I stand here today humbled by the task before us, grateful for the trust you have bestowed, mindful of the sacrifices borne by our ancestors. I thank President Bush for his service to our nation, as well as the generosity and cooperation he has shown throughout this transition.

Forty-four Americans have now taken the presidential oath. The words have been spoken during rising tides of prosperity and the still waters of peace. Yet, every so often the oath is taken amidst gathering clouds and raging storms. At these moments, America has carried on not simply because of the skill or vision of those in high office, but because We the People have remained faithful to the ideals of our forbearers, and true to our founding documents.

So it has been. So it must be with this generation of Americans.

That we are in the midst of crisis is now well understood. Our nation is at war, against a far-reaching network of violence and hatred. Our economy is badly weakened, a consequence of greed and irresponsibility on the part of some, but also our collective failure to make hard choices and prepare the nation for a new age. Homes have been lost; jobs shed; businesses shuttered. Our health care is too costly; our schools fail too many; and each day brings further evidence that the ways we use energy strengthen our adversaries and threaten our planet.

These are the indicators of crisis, subject to data and statistics. Less measurable but no less profound is a sapping of confidence across our land—a nagging fear that America's decline is inevitable, and that the next generation must lower its sights.

Today I say to you that the challenges we face are real. They are serious and they are many.

They will not be met easily or in a short span of time. But know this, America—they will be met. On this day, we gather because we have chosen hope over fear, unity of purpose over conflict and discord.

On this day, we come to proclaim an end to the petty grievances and false promises, the recriminations and worn out dogmas, that for far too long have strangled our politics.

We remain a young nation, but in the words of Scripture, the time has come to set aside childish things. The time has come to reaffirm our enduring spirit; to choose our better history; to carry forward that precious gift, that noble idea, passed on from generation to generation: the God-given promise that all are equal, all are free, and all deserve a chance to pursue their full measure of happiness.

In reaffirming the greatness of our nation, we understand that greatness is never a given. It must be earned. Our journey has never been one of short-cuts or settling for less. It has not been the path for the faint-hearted—for those who prefer leisure over work, or seek only the pleasures of riches and fame. Rather, it has been the risk-takers, the doers, the makers of things—

some celebrated but more often men and women obscure in their labor, who have carried us up the long, rugged path towards prosperity and freedom.

For us, they packed up their few worldly possessions and traveled across oceans in search of a new life.

For us, they toiled in sweatshops and settled the West; endured the lash of the whip and plowed the hard earth. (abcnews.go.com/Politics/Inauguration/president-obama-inaguration-speech-transcript/story?id=6689022)

A little history on Barack H. Obama:

Barack H. Obama is the 44th President of the United States.

His story is the American story—values from the heartland, a middle-class upbringing in a strong family, hard work and education as the means of getting ahead, and the conviction that a life so blessed should be lived in service to others.

With a father from Kenya and a mother from Kansas, President Obama was born in Hawaii on August 4, 1961. He was raised with help from his grandfather, who served in Patton's army, and his grandmother, who worked her way up from the secretarial pool to middle management at a bank.

After working his way through college with the help of scholarships and student loans, President Obama moved to Chicago, where he worked with a group of churches to help rebuild communities devastated by the closure of local steel plants.

He went on to attend law school, where he became the first African-American president of the *Harvard Law Review*. Upon graduation, he returned to Chicago to help lead a voter registration drive, teach constitutional law at the University of Chicago, and remain active in his community.

President Obama's years of public service are based around his unwavering belief in the ability to unite people around a politics of purpose. In the Illinois State Senate, he passed the first major ethics reform in 25 years, cut taxes for working families, and expanded health care for children and their parents. As a United States Senator, he reached across the aisle to pass groundbreaking lobbying reform, lock up the world's most dangerous weapons, and bring transparency to government by putting federal spending online.

He was elected the 44th President of the United States on November 4, 2008, and sworn in on January 20, 2009. He and his wife, Michelle, are the proud parents of two daughters, Malia, 10, and Sasha, 7. (obamawhitehouse. archives.gov/1600/presidents/barackobama)

February 20, 2009

Dear girls,

I'm writing this letter, copying most of it, regarding the economic crisis that the United States is going through. There is talk about it being like the Great Depression that took place in the late 1920s. I want you both to see how tough times are for people right now in our economy. This is a very trying time in your future and lives. We just elected a new president, Barack Obama, who will hopefully turn this crisis around. Here is a little history about the depression.

A Short History of the Great Depression

Great Depression

The Great Depression was the worst economic crisis in modern history, lasting from 1929 until the beginning of World War II in 1939. The causes of the Great Depression included slowing consumer demand, mounting consumer debt, decreased industrial production and the rapid and reckless expansion of the U.S. stock market. When the stock market crashed in October 1929, it triggered a crisis in the international economy, which was linked via the gold standard. A rash of bank failures followed in 1930, and as the Dust Bowl increased the number of farm fore-closures, unemployment topped 20 percent by 1933. Presidents Herbert Hoover and Franklin D. Roosevelt tried to stimulate the economy with a range of incentives including Roosevelt's New Deal programs, but ultimately it took the man-ufacturing production increases of World War II to end the Great Depression.

What Caused the Great Depression?

Throughout the 1920s, the U.S. economy expanded rapidly, and the nation's total wealth more than doubled between 1920 and 1929, a period dubbed "the Roaring Twenties."

The stock market, centered at the New York Stock Exchange on Wall Street in New York City, was the scene of reckless speculation, where everyone from millionaire tycoons to cooks and janitors poured their savings into stocks. As a result, the stock market underwent rapid expansion, reaching its peak in August 1929.

By then, production had already declined and unemployment had risen, leaving stock prices much higher than their actual value. Additionally, wages at that time were low, consumer debt was proliferating, the agricultural sector of the economy was struggling due to drought and falling food prices and banks had an excess of large loans that could not be liquidated.

The American economy entered a mild recession during the summer of 1929, as consumer spending slowed and unsold goods began to pile up, which in turn slowed factory production. Nonetheless, stock prices continued to rise and, by the fall of that year, had reached stratospheric levels that could not be justified by expected future earnings.

Stock Market Crash of 1929

On October 24, 1929, as nervous investors began selling overpriced shares en masse, the stock market crash that some had feared happened at last. A record 12.9 million shares were traded that day, known as "Black Thursday."

Five days later, on October 29, or "Black Tuesday," some 16 million shares were traded after another wave of panic swept Wall Street. Millions of shares ended up worthless, and those investors who had bought stocks "on margin" (with borrowed money) were wiped out completely.

As consumer confidence vanished in the wake of the stock market crash, the downturn in spending and investment led factories and other businesses to slow down production and begin firing their workers. For those who were lucky enough to remain employed, wages fell and buying power decreased.

Many Americans forced to buy on credit fell into debt, and the number of foreclosures and repossessions climbed steadily. The global adherence to the gold standard, which joined countries around the world in fixed currency exchange, helped spread economic woes from the United States throughout the world, especially in Europe.

Bank Runs and the Hoover Administration

Despite assurances from President Herbert Hoover and other leaders that the crisis would run its course, matters continued to get worse over the next three years. By 1930, 4 million Americans looking for work could not find it; that number had risen to 6 million in 1931.

Meanwhile, the country's industrial production had dropped by half. Bread lines, soup kitchens, and rising numbers of homeless people became more and more common in America's towns and cities. Farmers couldn't afford to harvest their crops and were forced to leave them rotting in the fields while people elsewhere starved. In 1930, severe droughts in the Southern Plains brought high winds and dust from Texas to Nebraska, killing people, livestock, and crops. The "Dust Bowl" inspired a mass migration of people from farmland to cities in search of work.

In the fall of 1930, the first of four waves of banking panics began, as large numbers of investors lost confidence in the solvency of their banks and demanded deposits in cash, forcing banks to liquidate loans in order to supplement their insufficient cash reserves on hand.

Bank runs swept the United States again in the spring and fall of 1931 and the fall of 1932, and by early 1933 thousands of banks had closed their doors.

In the face of this dire situation, Hoover's administration tried supporting failing banks and other institutions with government loans; the idea was that the banks in turn would loan to businesses, which would be able to hire back their employees.

FDR and the Great Depression

Hoover, a Republican who had formerly served as U.S. secretary of commerce, believed that government should not directly intervene in the economy and that it did not have the responsibility to create jobs or provide economic relief for its citizens.

In 1932, however, with the country mired in the depths of the Great Depression and some 15 million people unemployed, Democrat Franklin

D. Roosevelt won an overwhelming victory in the presidential election.

By Inauguration Day (March 4, 1933), every U.S. state had ordered all remaining banks to close at the end of the fourth wave of banking panics, and the U.S. Treasury didn't have enough cash to pay all government workers. Nonetheless, FDR (as he was known) projected a calm energy and optimism, famously declaring "the only thing we have to fear is fear itself."

Roosevelt took immediate action to address the country's economic woes, first announcing a four-day "bank holiday" during which all banks would close so that Congress could pass reform legislation and reopen those banks determined to be sound. He also began addressing the public directly over the radio in a series of talks, and these so-called "fireside chats" went a long way toward restoring public confidence.

During Roosevelt's first 100 days in office, his administration passed legislation that aimed to stabilize industrial and agricultural production, create jobs, and stimulate recovery.

In addition, Roosevelt sought to reform the financial system, creating the Federal Deposit Insurance Corporation (FDIC) to protect depositors' accounts and the Securities and Exchange Commission (SEC) to regulate the stock market and prevent abuses of the kind that led to the 1929 crash.

The New Deal: A Road to Recovery

Among the programs and institutions of the New Deal that aided in recovery from the Great Depression was the Tennessee Valley Authority

(TVA), which built dams and hydroelectric projects to control flooding and provide electric power to the impoverished Tennessee Valley region, and the Works Progress Administration (WPA), a permanent jobs program that employed 8.5 million people from 1935 to 1943.

When the Great Depression began, the United States was the only industrialized country in the world without some form of unemployment insurance or social security. In 1935, Congress passed the Social Security Act, which for the first time provided Americans with unemployment, disability, and pensions for old age.

After showing early signs of recovery beginning in the spring of 1933, the economy continued to improve throughout the next three years, during which real GDP (adjusted for inflation) grew at an average rate of 9 percent per year.

A sharp recession hit in 1937, caused in part by the Federal Reserve's decision to increase its requirements for money in reserve. Though the economy began improving again in 1938, this second severe contraction reversed many of the gains in production and employment and prolonged the effects of the Great Depression through the end of the decade.

Depression-era hardships fueled the rise of extremist political movements in various European countries, most notably that of Adolf Hitler's Nazi regime in Germany. German aggression led war to break out in Europe in 1939, and the WPA turned its attention to strengthening the military infrastructure of the United States, even as the country maintained its neutrality.

African Americans in the Great Depression

One-fifth of all Americans receiving federal relief during the Great Depression were Black, most in the rural South. But farm and domestic work, two major sectors in which Black workers were employed, were not included in the 1935 Social Security Act, meaning there was no safety net in times of uncertainty. Rather than fire domestic help, private employers could simply pay them less without legal repercussions. And those relief programs for which African Americans were eligible on paper were rife with discrimination in practice since all relief programs were administered locally.

Despite these obstacles, Roosevelt's "Black Cabinet," led by Mary McLeod Bethune, ensured nearly every New Deal agency had a Black advisor. The number of African Americans working in government tripled.

Women in the Great Depression

There was one group of Americans who actually gained jobs during the Great Depression: Women. From 1930 to 1940, the number of employed women in the United States rose 24 percent from 10.5 million to 13 million Though they'd been steadily entering the workforce for decades, the financial pressures of the Great Depression drove women to seek employment in ever greater numbers as male breadwinners lost their jobs. The 22 percent decline in marriage rates between 1929 and 1939 also created an increase in single women in search of employment.

Women during the Great Depression had a strong advocate in First Lady Eleanor Roosevelt, who lobbied her husband for more women in office—like Secretary of Labor Frances Perkins, the first woman to ever hold a cabinet position.

Jobs available to women paid less but were more stable during the banking crisis: nursing, teaching, and domestic work. They were supplanted by an increase in secretarial roles in FDR's rapidly-expanding government. But there was a catch: over 25 percent of the National Recovery Administration's wage codes set lower wages for women, and jobs created under the WPA confined women to fields like sewing and nursing that paid less than roles reserved for men.

Married women faced an additional hurdle: By 1940, 26 states had placed restrictions known as marriage bars on their employment, as working wives were perceived as taking away jobs from able-bodied men—even if, in practice, they were occupying jobs men would not want and doing them for far less pay.

Great Depression Ends and World War II Begins

With Roosevelt's decision to support Britain and France in the struggle against Germany and the other Axis Powers, defense manufacturing geared up, producing more and more private-sector jobs.

The Japanese attack on Pearl Harbor in December 1941 led to America's entry into World War II, and the nation's factories went back into full production mode.

This expanding industrial production, as well as widespread conscription beginning in 1942, reduced the unemployment rate to below its pre-Depression level. The Great Depression had ended at last, and the United States turned its attention to the global conflict of World War II. (www.history.com/topics/great-depression/great-depression-history)

I hope things turn around with this new president in charge. We, personally, have not been hit with financial breakdown yet, but Daddy's job was in jeopardy at one point, and Kasi's preschool was in jeopardy as well. The college was trying to cut back programs to save some money, but these programs were presented to the board and not cut after all. Mommy's job was not at risk, but parts of our general childcare programs were cut. This affects most of the working class who need childcare while the parents are at work.

The economic problems have affected Grandpa and Grandma hard. They were having trouble finding decent jobs that paid decent wages. We've been trying to help them out a little and buy them food and pay some of their bills for them.

Grandpa was talking about moving back to Oklahoma because he was getting deeper into debt living here, but if he moved, we would probably never see him again. He found a job driving a city bus, which has given him a lot of hours, but it was hard on him to get there.

Grandma has not found a consistent job other than working for Kasi's school, which doesn't pay much, but she is still driving a school bus for the district part-time. They are getting by, but it is a struggle for them.

It appears the economy has not really affected us as a family though. We still take you girls out to do activities and go out to eat on the weekends. We pay our bills and do a lot of things as a family, but our credit cards are adding up as well. We need to cut down on our spending, in case one of us does lose our job. I guess we can look at it as we are helping our economy out by still spending money. All we can really be is thankful that we have each other and our health. We love you girls very much and hope your future does not run into an economic crisis because of our generational decisions.

Love,
Mom

February 28, 2009

Dear Kendall,

This month was special for you and sissy. They had the Father/Daughter Dance this month, and both you and Kasi got to go with your Daddy. Mommy stayed home while you three had a date together. You saw a lot of your friends there and danced with them as well. You all had a really good time. You even got to see some of your friends that you hadn't seen in a long time. You both danced a lot with Daddy as well.

Being that February is the month for LOVE because of Valentine's Day, you had a spirit day the day before Valentine's Day. You were supposed to wear red.

This month is also known for Presidents' Break. You had a week off for the president's birthdays, Lincoln and Washington. For your break, you went to the Recreation Center.

Monday	Tuesday	Wednesday	Thursday	Friday
This day was closed for everyone	Ice-skating	Grand Sierra in Reno	Movie	Swimming

You have been taking spelling tests at school. You get a list of words at the beginning of the week, and by Friday, you take the test. You got a 100 percent on your first test. We were so proud of you that we took you out to dinner and you got to pick the place. You wanted to go to Orchid, Thai food. The following week, you got another 100 percent. Pretty soon, you were getting to pick the restaurant all the time because you were getting great scores on your tests.

We started basketball this month. You are on an all-boys team. In fact, you are the only girl in the boys' league. There are four groups of just girls, and the boys are separate. It's no coed teams this year. You did well too. You even pushed one boy onto the court to get the ball from him. You held your own, that is for sure. You made a lot of baskets.

Love,
Mom

March 29, 2009

Dear Kendall,

You have been playing great basketball. You have been shooting a lot of baskets. This year, instead of changing you from team to team, you have been on the same team in the same place on the court. There are just about three to four people on your team that are pretty good and shoot baskets, and you are one of them. The other good kid on your team is Andrew. He's one of the coach's sons. You can hold your own in the all-boys team.

Basketball didn't go very long this year. It was only on Saturdays for five weeks. This was your second year playing. You get a jersey and a nice basketball to keep.

We are going to try baseball this year. We've talked about it, but you have never played. We could either sign you up for T-ball or with a pitching machine. I thought T-ball was easier for you, so I picked the more challenging one for you. You are excited about it. My goal as your mom is to get you to try as many sports as you are willing to try. As you would say, "I'm not a tomboy. I'm a sporty girl." You say that Kasi is a tomboy because she likes brown and wears more pants instead of wearing pink skirts. At this point in time, she's too whiney to be a tomboy.

You have another break from school. This month, it's spring break. You went to the Recreation Center again. You usually say that you don't want to go to the Recreation Center, but once you go, you have so much fun. You basically get to do all the activities you want at a cheaper rate than what we would pay if we took you on our own. I tell you that you can go to work for me, and I'll go to the Recreation Center then. I would rather be out doing something fun instead of working.

On Wednesday, you had ice-skating this week, and it just so happened that it was a free ice-skating day, so after work, I took you and Kasi ice-skating, so you went almost all day. You are doing great on the ice. You are skating faster and not falling so much. Kasi as well. This was her second time skating. She used the walker for the beginning but soon wanted to try it to be just like you, and she was skating by herself. I hope she follows your lead in sports and is talented in anything she tries. You are a good lead to follow.

We took you both to a fundraiser concert for the American Cancer Society. It was amazing, AfroFlow. We even bought a CD of their music. You went up on stage with them, and Kasi fell asleep because she was so tired. I was surprised, too, because it was so loud in there. Their music is addictive and has a great rhythm.

> *AfroFlow* is a musical group heavily influenced by African beats through drums, spoken word, and call and response. The group started the Afroflow tour in 2006. They have partnered with the American Cancer Society (ACS) to speak out against the tobacco industry and to reach out to young adults about the dangers of tobacco use. The group consists of Mike-E, DJ Invisible, Kenny Watson, and Sowande Keita. (en.wikipedia.org/wiki/Afroflow)

You had breakfast with Daddy scheduled at school this month. You and Daddy got to eat breakfast with all the other kids and their dads. You were so excited to have your Daddy come to school with you.

Another spirit day at school. This one was crazy hair day. We put about five ponytails in your hair all over your head. You got a toy for participating in the day as well.

Jerra, your friend from school, had a birthday party in Reno. She invited three friends to go with her, and you were one of them. She also took Addie and Maya. There is a store in the mall down there where you all got makeup and were able to sing to music. On the way down to Reno, you got car sick. Jerra's mom, Rita, took you to her mother-in-law's house to clean you up, so you missed part of the party. Once you were feeling better, Rita took you to join the girls. You still had fun despite getting sick. You brought home makeup and a Girly Girl shirt. You girls get together and decide to all wear your shirts on the same day to school so that you all match. You have a pretty good group of friends that you play and hang out with through school.

St. Patrick's Day! We made traps to try and catch a leprechaun. We never did catch him, but he did leave his footprints and some cold candy coins. He left green pee in the toilet and tore the house apart looking for his pot of gold. I guess he did the same at school. You, of course, wore green to school.

You got your first report card this month. You did an excellent job. You are doing so well in school. Ms. Hood is very proud of you as well. You have received almost all your spelling tests and math tests back with 100 percent. We are all very proud of you. Ms. Hood says that you are warming up in class more and that you are talking and participating in class a lot more than last year. Math is your favorite subject so far.

I love you, baby girl.

Love,
Mom

April 25, 2009

Dear Kendall,

April Fool's Day was fun. I found a recipe on the internet for meat loaf cupcakes and made them for dinner. You were both looking at it like there was something wrong. I told you that you were having cupcakes for dinner. The mashed potatoes on top were dark in color, and I guess they looked a little scary. I had a good laugh. They tasted good though.

If you did well at the school where you are, you were able to eat lunch with your principal, Mr. Galles. You were so excited to eat lunch with your principal.

There was a spirit day at school this month. This one was for literacy. You dressed up in a pirate costume for *Pirates of the Caribbean*.

We decided to go to Sebastopol for Easter this year. This year, Mema is turning eighty years old, and so it was a birthday party as well. You were able to play with your friends from the year before. You decorated eggs and hunted for them and found Easter baskets. You both had fun. We took Chili and Paintbrush with us. Paintbrush, I think, remembered where we were because he just wanted to run and run. He loves it there. Chili was just tired from trying to keep up with him. They slept all the way home. They even slept a couple of days after once we got them home. Grandpa's birthday was on Easter Day. We called him to wish him a happy birthday. He had to work, so he was not able to go with us.

There was another breakfast at your school, but instead of dad, it was with mom. Moms gathered to eat breakfast with their kids at school. We sat with Maya and her mom.

You are playing baseball better. Now that you understand the game a little more and can hit the ball better, you are getting the hang of it. Even the coaches have come to you telling you that you are doing well. They even said they think you should be on another team, an older team, because you are playing so well. I don't think you want to play baseball next year. At least you tried it though. You are the only girl on the team again. Andrew that was on your team for basketball is on your team for baseball. His dad is your coach.

There was an Earth Day event scheduled at MontBleu this month. We went to see what they had to do. We got a few pine trees to plant and some wildflower seeds. We planted them all in our yard. You both helped me dig the holes. After we dug holes and planted them, we watered them.

There was a bounce house that you both played on. We made pinecone bird feeders with peanut butter and bird seeds. Usually, I put the peanut butter on the pinecones, and then you guys roll them into the bird seeds to cover it up. We hang them in front of the house when we get home. You came home from school one day and asked me, "What does this mean?" You used your hands to sign the letters W-E-M-L in sign language.

I said that I didn't know. "What Ever Major Loser." I asked you where you learned that. You told me someone from school.

I asked you what this meant. I used my hands to sign the letters W-E-B-L in sign language. "What Ever Big Loser." I got you back. I just laughed.

You even got Kasi saying it now. It's funny to hear you both say it and do it with attitude.

Love,
Mom

May 11, 2009

Dear girls,

This month so far has been great! Kasi just had her fourth birthday, and we decided not to throw either one of you a party. Instead, this year, we went to...yep, you guessed it. Disneyland.

We took everyone to Venice beach and cruised around down by the beach to see the street activities. We saw a couple of street performers and then off to Marina del Rey. We picked up seashells and put our feet in the ocean. It was a little chilly, so we didn't stay long. We ate dinner at this great Italian restaurant, C&O Trattoria, I always want to eat at when we go to Los Angeles. We had them sing happy birthday to Kasi, but they sang in Italian, so she had no clue what they were singing.

We surprised you girls this year. We never mentioned to you that we were going to Disneyland. We told you that we were going to Los Angels to see family and celebrate Kasi's birthday. Normally, when you go to Los Angeles though, it's usually you girls and Daddy. On this trip, Grandma and I both came along.

We stayed at Angelica and Israel's house the first night we arrived. The next day, we said that we were going to go to a hotel instead to stay because it was too crowded with all of us staying at their house. We went to Downtown Disney the night we checked into the hotel. The first thing you both saw was the swimming pool. You both wanted to go swimming the next day, and I told you that I didn't know if we would have time because we had a very busy weekend planned for us.

The next morning, we took the shuttle from the hotel and said that we were going to Downtown Disney again. Kendall wanted to go on a roller coaster. She saw one from where we were the night before. I told you that there were no roller coasters at Downtown Disney. I told you if you wanted to pretend you were on a roller coaster to put your arms up in the air when the shuttle went over a speed bump to get the full effect.

We walked into Disneyland, and we were standing right in front of the Mickey Mouse head made of flowers in the background. I leaned over and said, "Happy birthday, girls. You're in Disneyland." You were both in shock and didn't say much. Our journey began from there. We wanted strollers for the both of you so that we wouldn't have to carry you both when you got tired, but we ended up carrying you a lot of the time anyway. You can't take the strollers in the lines for the rides. Grandma bought you both autograph books so that you could get autographs from the characters in the park.

We got a three-day park hopper ticket package with a four-night stay in the hotel. We were planning on spending two days at Disneyland and one day in California Adventure. Angelica, Israel, Abuelita, Diego, and Mariana met up with us on Saturday in Disneyland.

We started in Tomorrowland: Autopia, Buzz Lightyear, Astro Blasters, Finding Nemo Submarine Voyage, "Honey, I shrunk the Audience,: Space Mountain, and Star Tours.

We let you girls drive the cars on the Autopia. Good thing they were on tracks because you drive crazy. Buzz Lightyear was a ride where we shot at targets, and it kept score for us at the end of all the targets we hit. On the Nemo ride, we went aboard a submarine underwater. It was very cool to see the ocean life below. "Honey, I shrunk the Audience" was a 3D experience where it made the audience look as though we were as big as a shoebox. It was all make believe though. Space Mountain was too much for Mommy, so Kendall, Daddy, Angelica, and Israel went on this ride together. Star Tours was one of the first rides Daddy wanted to go on because it's like Star Wars. We know how Daddy likes his Star Wars. One of the other attractions was the Jedi training. Daddy wanted to do this, but they were only picking kids out of the audience. He was so mesmerized that I took a picture of him with his mouth wide open.

We walked through Sleeping Beauty's Castle to Fantasyland. This is where we went on: "It's a Small World," King Arthur's Carrousel, Matterhorn Bobsleds, Peter Pan's Flight, Pinocchio's Daring Journey, Snow White's Scary Adventure, and the Storybook Land Canal Boats.

I'm glad that you girls are not huge girly girl princess fans. There was a boutique where they would dress you up as a princess, put makeup on you, and do your hair for only a whopping $250 or more. We walked out of this store quickly. Kasi has been practicing "It's a Small World" for Multicultural Day at school, so this was a treat to see the ride.

We were all singing the song while going through it. Mommy gets sick on carrousels, and so Daddy had to take you both on this ride. I couldn't even watch you going around on it. The Matterhorn Bobsleds was a wet roller coaster. We sat in a bobsled, trailing through a mountain and into water. You both liked getting wet. On Peter Pan, you journey through town flying on a little ship overlooking the town below you. Pinocchio's ride has you swallowed up by the whale through your travels. Snow White takes the apple from the witch, but the dwarfs save her at the end. The Storybook Land Canal was a little boring for a ride. You coast on a boat through all the fairy-tale adventures in a miniature version while the driver of the boat tells a story. We can skip this ride next time we come.

We wanted to go on the roller coaster with water before it got too cold and late, so we walked all the way over to the other end of the park to Critter Country: Splash Mountain, Davey Crockett's Explorer Canoes, and the Many Adventures of Winnie the Pooh. We almost didn't get to ride Splash Mountain. The ride broke down while we were standing in a line for over an hour, it seemed like. Kasi's hands were up in the air the whole ride. We got a great picture of all of us coming down the waterfall. All our mouths were open wide. You both wanted to go again, but being that it took us forever to go the first time, we skipped it. The Davey Crockett Canoes was a ride I had never been on before. We had to use oars and paddle the whole ride. You both used little oars to help paddle. You didn't want to do this ride again; it was too much work. The Winnie Pooh Ride was short and sweet. We sat in a beehive for the ride. We did see Winnie Pooh and Tigger in front of the entrance, and you got pictures taken with them, but I thought we left the autograph books back at the hotel, so you didn't get their autographs. We went to the petting farm and petted some sheep. We tried to get Woody and

Jesse's autograph and picture while we were there in Critter Country, but it was for private guests only. Kasi was so bummed. These are her favorite characters. In fact, Kasi received a $60 gift certificate for celebrating her birthday, and she chose to get Woody, Jesse, Buzz Lightyear, Bullseye stuffed animals, and a Jesse cowgirl hat. She's been sleeping with them almost every night since we've came home.

I really wanted to see the Haunted Mansion before the night was over. Off to New Orleans Square to see the Haunted Mansion and the Pirates of the Caribbean.

These are my two favorite rides, besides "It's a Small World." You were both scared at first because you didn't know what was going to happen, and they were both dark rides. We ended up going through the Haunted Mansion twice. There are ghosts at the end of the ride that sit in the carts with you. You could see them in the mirrors as we went by. You were both looking in the mirrors and looking at each other. It was sort of funny. You were both wondering how they were sitting with you in the mirror, but not in the carts.

Adventureland was a quick site to see with the Enchanted Tiki Room, Indiana Jones, and Tarzan's Treehouse.

In the Tiki Room, there were birds and totem poles singing. There was a fake thunderstorm and rain along the windows. You both liked this feature. Kasi could not go on the Indiana Jones ride because she was too short, so Daddy, Grandma, and Kendall all went on the ride together. Kendall liked it. I'm glad I didn't go because I think I would have gotten sick from the visual effects. Tarzan's Treehouse was a large tree house that you just walked through. It was fun for the both of you.

Toontown is for smaller children. It has rides like Chip 'n Dale Treehouse, Donald's Boat, Gadget's Go Coaster, Goofy's Playhouse, Mickey's House, Minnie's House, and Roger Rabbit's Car Toon Spin.

All Toontown looks animated and cartoon décor. Most of Toontown is small rides for smaller children. You still had fun. Chip 'n Dale's Treehouse was another walk-through tree house. Donald's Boat was more of a playground that you climb on. The Gadget Go Coaster was a little roller coaster that went around the track just once.

It was a short ride, but it was fun. Goofy's Playhouse was another walk-through. Kendall laid down on the couch, and Kasi played the piano. We walked through Mickey and Minnie's houses as well. You were able to get a picture with Minnie at her house. The Roger Rabbit Car Toon Spin was a ride that went through in a taxi. This was a fun ride, but a very long wait. Toontown had cars and items that you could play with just in town. You played in the jail and tried to lift the barbells.

The only thing we did in Frontierland was ride the Big Thunder Mountain Railroad. You both liked this roller coaster, and we got a little wet on it. We went on this ride twice. Diego cried while we waited in line with him, but we made him go, and he had fun after all.

These are the characters that you were able to get pictures with: Goofy, Pluto, Minnie Mouse, Mickey Mouse, Buzz Lightyear, Cruella de Vil, Chip 'n Dale, Winnie the Pooh, Tigger, Mary Poppins, and Bert.

We even went on the Disneyland Railroad to go from one part of town to the other, just to save us some walking time.

We went to California Adventure on the last day of our trip. There were little pieces of California throughout the park. When you walk into the park, you walk under the Golden Gate Bridge.

The first ride that you wanted to go on was the California Screamin' because the park had just opened, and we knew the lines were going to be long, so we went straight to Paradise Pier.

Paradise Pier: Toy Story Midway Mania, California Screamin', Mulholland Madness, and Jumpin' Jellyfish.

Kasi could not go on California Screamin' because she was too little, so Daddy, Grandma, and Kendall all went on it first. Kasi and I watched and ate ice cream. When you finished the ride, Daddy, Kendall, and I went on it. This was the day I didn't take any motion sickness medicine, and sure enough, I got sick. I was lying down for over an hour while you all went around the park. It was not fun for me. I ended up finding a store that sold the medicine, and I bought some so that I would be able to go with you all and not feel sick all day. This was Kendall's favorite ride in this park. She wanted to go again. I laid down on a bench while you all waited in line to go through the Toy Story Midway Mania. I was going to go, but when I stood in line for just less than five minutes, I had to go lay down again. So you all went without me. It was in 3D, so you all wore glasses. I guess it was a lot like the Buzz Lightyear ride. Potato head was at the front of the ride talking and moving around. He was cool to watch. Mulholland Madness was a small roller coaster ride, which Kasi could not go on, and so I stayed with her while you all went on this ride. Kasi could go on the Jumpin' Jellyfish ride, so Grandma went with Kendall and Daddy went with Kasi. Kasi went on this ride twice.

A Bug's Land: It's Tough to Be a Bug!, Bountiful Valley Farm, Flik's Flyers, Heimlich's Chew Chew Train, and Tuck and Roll Drive 'Em Buggies.

We cruised over to A Bug's Land from Paradise Pier. It's Tough to Be a Bug was great! This was a 3D video about being a bug and how hard life is. During the show, the seats felt like bugs crawling underneath our butts and behind our backs. The audience screamed. We were then squirted with water in our faces as a bug was spitting at us. It was very entertaining. Bountiful Valley Farm had an irrigation system that you both played in and got soaking wet. It was like giant sprinklers that all the kids were running through. It was hot outside, so it felt good to get a little wet. You both got too wet and cried afterwards because you were cold. Flik's Flyers were hot-air balloons made of leaves that spun around and around. It was a quick ride. Daddy took both of you on the ride. Heimlich's Chew Chew Train takes you on a journey to find food. You can even smell some of the foods along the ride. Tuck and Roll Drive 'Em Buggies are bug bumper cars. You and Kasi both drove the cars, and I bumped into both while you were trying to drive.

Golden State—Grizzly Peak Recreation Area and Grizzly River Run

The Grizzly River Run had a height limit on it, and so Kasi could not go on it. She ended up going to the Grizzly Peak Recreation Area and playing in the playground.

236

Grandma, Kendall, and I went on the ride first and got wet. It's a giant raft ride that sends you down an abandoned mine and rushing on a river with rapids, caverns, and waterfalls. When we got off the ride, it was a ten-minute wait, and Art and Kendall went on it. The rest of us sat on the rocks to watch you come down and get us wet. It was getting cold though.

Hollywood Back Pictures Lot: Monsters, Inc., Mike and Sulley to the Rescue!, Muppet Vision 3D, Disney Animation (Turtle Talk with Crush, Animation Academy, Character Close-Up, and the Sorcerer's Workshop.)

Monsters, Inc. was a ride in a taxi through the safe return of Boo. It was like a movie. The Muppet Vision 3D was more of a video, but there were some pieces of the show that were in front of the screen. There were penguins conducting the orchestra in front and a cannonball that blew up part of the wall. We went to the Disney Animation Theater, where the interactive adventure takes on an art form. This is a behind-the-scenes peek into how animation forms into your favorite characters. The interactive experience included: **Animation Academy**—learn the secrets of how to draw a classic Disney character with a hands-on lesson from a Disney artist! **Sorcerer's Workshop**—learn about this imaginative art form by entering the three magical realms of the world of animation, wherein you interact, play, and create your own animation! **Turtle Talk with Crush**—get face-to-fin with Crush, the totally awesome sea turtle from the Disney/Pixar film *Finding Nemo* for a live conversation in this digital interactive experience. Crush was very cool. You both asked him questions, and he replied to you through the screen.

One of the best parts of Disney's California Adventures was the Pixar parade. It was all the recent Pixar movies from *Monsters, Inc.*, *Cars*, *Toy Story*, *Incredibles*, *Finding Nemo*, and *Bug's Life*. You both really enjoyed this!

This was the best family trip we have ever taken. It was a long weekend for how much we did, but it was worth it. We covered a lot of the parks and didn't fight with each other. It was great to see the looks on your faces with some of the attractions we covered. I hope this was a birthday to never forget. We are just glad that we were able to take you both on this fabulous trip. We hope to do this again. You both have asked when we are going again. Kasi asked if we could go to Disneyland tomorrow, like it's just around the corner from our house.

We love you both very much.

Love,
Mom

May 31, 2009

Dear Kendall,

We did have your birthday celebration, but it was in Disneyland with the family and not at school with all your friends. Happy birthday, baby girl. Grandma took you both to McDonald's, and you got an ice cream. She stuck a candle in it and sang to you.

Grandma's birthday was this month as well as Mother's Day. We got her flowers, and all went to breakfast.

Kasi had Multicultural Day at the college. Kasi couldn't decide if she wanted to dress up as a soccer player from Mexico or in a hula costume and say that she was from Hawaii. She finally decided on the hula costume, but when she introduced herself, she said something else: "My name is Kasi, and I'm from Mexico." We all laughed. She didn't even realize it until after she said it. I guess she was nervous with all those people in the audience staring at her. We let you take the day off from school so that you can participate in the event. You were the soccer player from Mexico. You participated in the event with Kasi. One of the little girls in her class, Parker, wore a princess dress and announced that she was the Queen of England. She even waved her hand to everyone in the audience. This had everyone laughing. It was very funny and unexpected.

Mommy and Daddy were supposed to dance as well, but I didn't know if I was going to get the day off work or not, so Daddy danced with America instead. Everyone loved it when your daddy came up. He danced the Merengue and then did a line dance with the kids in the audience. He was a hit! Your daddy likes to be the center of attention.

You lost a tooth this month. You just love playing with them until they fall out once you know you have a tooth loose.

Mommy and Daddy celebrated their nine-year wedding anniversary this month. Nine years is a very long time.

There was an open house night at your school. You and I both went together. I talked to Ms. Hood, your teacher, and she adores you. I asked her about what teachers were going to be teaching next year, and she mentioned that she would like to keep you in her class next year if we didn't mind. She will be teaching another first and second grade combo class. She didn't know if she was still going to be there next year or not though. With all the budget cuts, her position might be one of the ones cut. I told her that we would love to have you in her class next year, but that she knows you very well, and we would let her decide who you would have as a teacher next year. You really would like to have Ms. Hood again as your teacher. You are getting comfortable with her and have blossomed in her class over the last two years.

I love you very much.

Love,
Mom

June 25, 2009

Dear girls,

The King of Pop, Michael Jackson, died suddenly today after suffering cardiac arrest. He was fifty. He started his debut at age eleven with his five brothers, the Jackson 5. Since 1982, he has become a single producer of many hit records. Michael started a dance called the moonwalk. Just to name a few of his major hits: "Thriller," "Don't Stop 'Til You Get Enough," "Rock with You," "Billie Jean," "The Girl Is Mine," "Smooth Criminal," "I Just Can't Stop Loving You," "Bad," "The Way You Make Me Feel," "Man in the Mirror," "Dirty Diana," "Black or White," "Remember the Time," "Butterflies," "You Rock My World," and "Cry."

Former Charlie's Angel Farrah Fawcett died today at age sixty-two after a long struggle with anal cancer, her spokesman told media organizations.

Fawcett's movie and TV roles after *Charlie's Angels* included *The Cannonball Run*, *The Burning Bed*, *Small Sacrifices*, *Extremities*, and *The Apostle*. Fawcett's swimsuit poster made her an icon in the 1970s. She and Ryan O'Neal have a son, Redmond, born in 1985.

Jackson death causes media scramble
By DAVID BAUDER
AP TELEVISION WRITER

NEW YORK—Two broadcast TV networks were already planning dueling prime-time specials on Farrah Fawcett's death Thursday. Then Michael Jackson died.

It forced an extraordinary scramble for news organizations from covering the death of an entertainment icon to another.

"What a sad, incredible...you couldn't write this," said a nonplussed Larry King on CNN, describing how his planned show on Fawcett was "blown out of the well" with Jackson's death. He sensed immediately what most news organizations did, that the Jackson story was bigger, because of both the surprise factor and the magnitude of his stardom.

ABC had planned an hour on Fawcett's death, a Barbara Walters special that had initially been scheduled for Friday but had been moved up earlier this week when word came that her condition was grave. NBC News, which last month had presented a show on Fawcett's fight against anal cancer, announced shortly after her death that it would do its own Fawcett special.

After Jackson's death, they became two-hour specials—one hour on each star. CBS also put together a quick hour mixing the stories.

"I think we should remember Michael Jackson as the great performer he was," Walters said.

Earlier, she had asked co-anchor Martin Bashir whether Jackson would be remembered more for his talent or his scandals. Bashir answered that it would be his music. But the special, perhaps because there was so little time to put it together, leaned heavily on tapes of old interviews with Bashir, Walters and Diane Sawyer that focused more on his oddities than what had brought him to prominence in the first place.

The cable news networks almost immediately began covering the story exclusively.

Fox News had twin crawls in urgent yellow at the bottom of its screen, one repeating "breaking news" and the other nuggets like: "MC Hammer tweets on Jackson death: 'I have no words.'"

Clips of Jackson performances and videos ran continuously as wallpaper, their quick camera cuts reminiscent of MTV in the 1980s, which lived off Jackson's hits. (www.sandiegouniontribune.com/sdut-us-michael-jackson-media-062509-2009jun25-story.html)

June 27, 2009

Dear Kendall,

There was an event called the Spring Fling at your school. There was also a talent show. Most of the talents were fifth graders though. There was dancing, singing, and magic. We all liked the song "Who Let the Dogs Out." It was more of a talent though. It was three girls holding up Hula-Hoops for their dog to jump through. We voted for this one at the end of the night.

Happy birthday, seven-year-old! Since we celebrated both yours and Kasi's birthday in Disneyland this year, we didn't do very much for your birthday. I let you take granola bars to school to share with your class so that they could sing to you.

You went on a field trip with your class. You went to Chevy's and the post office. Grandpa went with you. Daddy even dropped you off at Grandma and Grandpa's house so that he could take you to school. You wanted him to take you. You were excited. At Chevy's, you watched them make tortillas in the machine and handmade guacamole. You even ate guacamole. You like it so much; you ask for it at home. At the post office, you went in the back and watched how they sorted mail and what the process was for delivery.

You are getting better at baseball. You were the catcher at one of your games. You put all the gear on, pads, and face guard. You liked catching. You wanted to play the catcher again in another game, but they had to give everyone a turn.

You played an awesome game today. First you hit the ball over the pitcher in between first and second bases, and the second ball you hit over the pitcher again, but in between the second and third bases. The third hit went high in the air and fell short. Another time, you were covering third base, and a ball was coming at you. You ran up to it and turned around to get the other team member out on third base. You were incredible! Both of your coaches came up to you after the game and told you that they think you should be in a larger league with bigger kids.

We went to the college for the Day of the Young Child event. It was a bunch of booths spread out with different activities for kids to do. One booth took your pictures and fingerprints for free so that we have all your information on hand in case you get separated from us. Another booth was a bean bag toss that you won three goldfish from. There was a dental booth where you both got fluoride varnish on your teeth. There was coloring, water play, gymnastics, and games. We were there for a while.

You colored a picture of you and Juan together holding hands. You wrote, "I love Jnau and Jnau loves me. I love Jnau." I asked you what that meant, and you said that you liked each other. Only you spelled his name wrong, Juan. You hung it over your bed in your room.

For Father's Day, we took Daddy and Grandpa out for breakfast to celebrate. While we were at breakfast, we saw Katherine having breakfast with her daddy. They asked if you could come over to their house for a playdate after breakfast. You took the bikes out for a ride, played on their hover board, and went to the creek to play in the water. You had a good time.

I was off work all week to save money for childcare and to spend time with you. We went horseback riding, just the two of us. You've been asking to go for a long time. I remember why we don't do it very often. It's expensive.

You had a playdate and sleep over with Maya this week off as well. We all took our bikes and journeyed to the tennis courts and had ice cream. We took the dogs for a walk, and you both played outside.

We took Kasi out of school on the last day of our vacation to go mini golfing. We had a girl's day out. Grandpa met us at the golf course to watch you girls play. You didn't play very well though. You would hit the ball before it would even stop from the last time you hit it. Grandpa laughed. You both had fun, and that's all that mattered.

I love you.

Love,
Mom

June 29, 2009

Dear Kendall,

Well, you little monkey, you finally did it. You play on the monkey bars and act crazy sometimes, but today, your hand slipped while you were on the monkey bars, and you fell at the Recreation Center. You hit the back of your head on one of the foot bars, and they rushed you to the emergency room. You were wrapped up to a board, and your head was taped with a neck brace. The Recreation Center called me and Daddy. I called Grandma, and we all met you at the hospital. I was the last one to show up. I walked into your room to see you all strapped up, and I started crying. I always dread the day when I would have to walk into an emergency room to see you hurt. I didn't know to what extent you had hurt yourself. The doctor came in to examine you and took the wrapping off you to check your head, and you moved your head all about. She didn't think that you hurt your head very badly and just examined you. She said that if you didn't want to eat, started to vomit, or your head started to hurt you really bad later, to bring you back into the emergency room.

Head injuries can be severe. A person just died the other day from a head injury. He was on a plane, and they had to make an emergency landing. The front tires of the plane had blown, and they landed okay, but the luggage from the overhead compartment fell and hit him on the head. He was not feeling well towards the end of the day, and he died in his sleep of a head injury.

Sometimes you have no fear when it comes to hurting yourself. You'll keep going right after this. I don't think you know your limits. I'm always telling you to be careful, but I'm just the mom. What do I know?

You got to ride in an ambulance from the Recreation Center to the hospital. I asked you if the ambulance crew was cute to make you laugh. You were too busy crying and thinking of your head to even remember. I'm glad that you're okay. You sure know how to scare your family though.

I love you, baby girl.

Love,
Mom

July 31, 2009

Dear Kendall,

Summer has started, and you are going to be joining the Recreation Center Tadaka again.

Monday	Tuesday	Wednesday	Thursday	Friday
		Painting	Climbing wall	Swimming
Bike to gymnastics Swimming	Bike to gymnastics Ice-skating	Bike to gymnastics Climbing wall	Kickball Sand Harbor	Swimming
Off all week with Daddy				
Swimming	Bike to Chevy's for a tour	Pirate costume Climbing wall	Wild Island	Movie Ice-skating
Football Swimming	Soccer Snowflake for ice cream	Bike to mini golf	Northstar Skating Sand Harbor	Kickball Swimming

You are excited about going this summer because they do so many fun things with you. You are good at climbing walls. You climbed five out of six of the walls. The only reason why you didn't climb the last one is because it was too hard and a little scary for you. One of the leaders, Justin, told you that you were awesome.

You are starting to like swimming again. You didn't want to go for the longest time because you didn't want to wear a life jacket, but I insisted because they cannot keep an eye on you all the time. You can swim, but you're not a strong enough swimmer to be in the deep end by yourself. I'd like to put you in another swimming class, but we have not been able to yet.

You love gymnastics! I'd really like to put you in that instead, but it's a little pricey. When they have those fun days at the Recreation Center, I make sure to sign you up for those days first.

You also love ice-skating. Those are days that I sign you up as well. Another pricey sport you'd like to take.

You took a tour through Chevy's Restaurant again. You have already done this trip through your school. They made guacamole and tortillas for you all to eat. They also made tacos for you.

Wild Island is a water park down in Sparks, Nevada. They have strict rules about what you can and cannot take into the park. You are not able to take your own water bottles in the park. I was a little worried that being that it is superhot down there in the summer. You came back from that day very dehydrated. You ended up throwing up, and we took you to the emergency room thinking that you had heat stroke and you had strep throat. We found out a day later.

You went roller skating at NorthStar and went to see a play at Valhalla. You really enjoyed both of those. I guess the play was funny and you were laughing during most of the play.

Your friend Allon has been coming to the Recreation Center as well. You played with him on his first day back for the summer. You came home and said that you needed to find a guy your age. I asked you what you needed for a guy your age. I asked you about Allon because he is four months younger than you. You said that he was younger and that you needed to find one who was your age. I'm starting to worry about having the birds and the bees conversation with you. I don't feel that you are old enough yet to start talking to you about boys. I know that you chase them, and you have kissed them before, but it was more to bother them, not to have a boyfriend or anything like that.

Your Daddy has been taking college classes now for about seven to eight years, part-time to get his bachelor's degree in social science. He drove down to take a test for Spanish. He took the Spanish challenge test so that he would not have to take the foreign language classes to get his degree. He passed with 79 out of 80 correct. That was all he needed to pass and get his degree. I am so proud of your daddy. He even graduated with honors. He has worked very hard on getting his degree.

My grandfather was very good at building things. He made kayaks out of plywood and canvas. Uncle Jeff has them in his garage. Uncle Jeff, Auntie Tina, Daddy, Kasi, you, and me all went to Fallen Leaf Lake to go kayaking. You did so well. You went out by yourself, and you have such great arm and upper body strength that you were almost able to keep up with me. Kasi went out with me, and the three of us raced. Daddy and Auntie Tina do not know how to swim, so they tried it near the shore and did very well. We are planning to go out again before the end of summer.

I love you.

Love,
Mom

August 27, 2009

Dear girls,

This is an amazing story and discovery, heart-wrenching at the same time. I wanted you to know about this story because in real life, this does happen. If you are to ever be taken away from your daddy and me, I want you to never give up and hold on no matter what. Children are kidnapped all the time. Unfortunately, most of them have ended up dead, but there are those special cases where the child is kept alive, sometimes tortured though. Kidnappings do happen, and I have feared this happening to the both of you before. I'm sure that most parents have had that fear before. This story broke out in South Lake Tahoe when I was a freshman in high school. Here are some pictures of what Jaycee Lee looked like when she was kidnapped.

Jaycee Dugard Found after 18 Years, Kidnap Suspect Allegedly Fathered Her Kids

August 27, 2009

A girl who was snatched off the street 18 years ago has been found, and the man-and-wife team that allegedly grabbed her has been arrested and charged with kidnapping and rape, officials said today.

The identity of Jaycee Lee Dugard, now 29, was revealed when she accompanied Phillip Garrido for questioning by his California parole officer. Garrido, a convicted kidnapper and rapist, also was accompanied by his wife Nancy and two young children that Garrido said were his.

Undersheriff Fred Kollar said in a news conference that Jaycee was the mother of the

251

two young children who had been fathered by Garrido.

Jaycee, who Garrido had renamed Allissa, was reunited with her mother Terry Probyn today, and the mother told ABC News that her daughter had been held against her will all these years and confined in a box in the back of the Garrido's house.

Kollar said that Jaycee had been held captive at a house in Antioch, Calif., since the day she was abducted and none of their neighbors ever knew.

He described the location as a "hidden back yard" within a larger yard that was arranged in such a way "to isolate the victims from outside contact."

Entrance to the secret yard was guarded by a 6-foot-tall fence, tall trees, and a tarp, he said.

Kollar said Jaycee and the two children lived a series of sheds, including one that was sound-proofed and that could only be opened from the outside. In addition, there were two tents in the yard.

"None of the children had ever gone to school, they had never gone to a doctor," Kollar said. "They were kept in complete isolation."

When asked about Jaycee's condition, the undersheriff said, "She is in good health, but living in a backyard for 18 years does take its toll."

Jaycee was with her mother today along with her two children, ages 11 and 15.

Garrido had been called in for questioning by his parole officer after being alerted by University of California-Berkeley campus security that Garrido was acting suspiciously.

When Garrido showed up for his grilling, there was difficulty in establishing the identity of everyone with him, said Scott Kernan, undersecretary for operations of California's Department of Corrections and Rehabilitation.

Under questioning, Garrido admitted to having kidnapped Dugard when she was 11 years old.

"There is nothing to indicate this was anything other than a stranger abduction," Kollar said. "No connection to the family. They literally snatched her off the streets."

Officers were convinced that Garrido was telling the truth when he and Jaycee told them details that only the kidnapper and victim would know, Kollar said.

Both Phillip Garrido, who is a 58-year-old registered sex offender, and Nancy Garrido, 54, are being held on $1 million bail, charged with kidnapping to commit rape.

The stunning news that Jaycee was alive and had been found elated Jaycee's parents.

"I had personally given up hope," her stepfather Carl Probyn said. "I had just hoped for a recovery" and to find the people responsible.

Instead, he said, "I've actually won the lotto."

But as the day wore on and details emerged of Jaycee's ordeal, Probyn became distraught.

Breaking down in tears, Probyn told ABC News, "My girl has no proper schooling, and I don't even know what shape she is in. I don't know if she was treated like an animal.... This is so horrific, I don't believe it." (abcnews.go.com/US/jaycee-lee-dugard-found-family-missing-girl-located/story?id=8426124)

I love you girls so very much. I would do anything to find you and hope this never happens to either one of you.

Love,
Mom

August 31, 2009

Dear Kendall,

You are still in the swing of summer and attending the Recreation Center. You are only going to attend for the first two weeks this month because Daddy is off the last two and he's taking you and Kasi to Los Angeles for part of it.

Monday	Tuesday	Wednesday	Thursday	Friday
Fear Factory Swimming	Donner Lake Lunch provided	Bike to Valhalla Shakespeare Swimming	Fear Factor Swimming	Fear Factor Swimming
Museum Swimming	Wall climbing	Bike to Pope Beach	Wild Island Lunch provided	Museum Swimming

We had soccer fun day. We found out that Mommy is coaching both you and Kasi's teams this season along with co-coaches. Luckily, you are on the same fields and close to the same times. You know most of your team. We have Olivia Craig, Katherine Dolan, Evelyn George, Maya Harvey, Taylor Rae Krider, Malia Lyons, Jerra McLaughlin, and Olivia Russell. You are going to miss the first two practices and your first game because you'll be in Los Angeles.

We got our uniforms, which are different from the last couple years. You have tank tops this year and vibrant colors—pink, black, and white. The team picked out the name Pink Panthers. We got an airbrushed banner this year, and it turned out very nice.

We signed up for Netflix. This is a program that is online. You sign up for so many movies a month, and they mail them to you. When you are done with the movie, you mail it back. We've been able to find old movies that Mommy and Daddy used to watch when we were kids, like *Smurfs, Fraggle Rock, Muppets Transformers,* and *The Love Bug.*

The Country Fair at St. Theresa's had its second annual community event this month. They had rides, slides, and games with performances by dancers and gymnasts. I think your favorite part is the big bouncy slide.

On other family topics. Mommy hasn't been feeling well for some time now, and I decided to go see a doctor about it. My ears have been plugged up, and I get a lot of headaches. I have been to our regular doctor, and they said that my ears are fine and that they are not plugged up. It hurts so sleep, and I feel like I'm in a bubble all the time, like my ears won't pop when you normally change in elevation. I went to see an ear, nose, and throat specialist. They thought it might be allergies, so they did some allergy tests on me, and I found out that I really do not have allergies.

I also did a sleep study to see if I had sleep apnea. (Sleep apnea means that you often stop breathing for ten seconds or longer during sleep. The problem can be mild to severe, based on the number of times each hour that you stop breathing or how often your lungs don't get enough air. This may happen from five to fifty times an hour.) I was having trouble sleeping and was snoring loud and would wake up feeling more tired than when I went to sleep. I have not received the results on this study yet.

I have also been having a lot of anxiety. (Anxiety is a state of apprehension, uncertainty, and fear resulting from the anticipation of a realistic or fantasized threatening event or situation, often impairing physical and psychological functioning.) I got medicine for this as well. I felt crazy and having weird dreams. I felt like I was on some sort of drug that was making me think and move quickly. This was also not helping my sleep as well. I would wake up in the middle of the night, and my mind just started thinking and would not stop.

I am trying to get some help to figure out how to be a little more normal.

Mommy and Daddy are also having some trouble in our marriage. Daddy has a friend that I think crossed the line between friend and more. He never cheated on the family, but I was just afraid with how much time they were spending with one another that it might get to that point, and I put my foot down and forbid them to have a personal relationship anymore. The problem is that they work together, and she has a son that you really like to play with. I don't believe they talk anymore. I didn't really mean for them to not be friends, but it was all or nothing. We can't have it both ways. I love your Daddy very much and want to keep our family together. You could say that I had a jealous moment in our lives and felt threatened by their relationship. Your daddy is a good man, and I would hate to lose him over an overseen mishap from not paying attention.

There is just too much going on at once, and it feels very overwhelming sometimes. We are doing better now since this all happened, but we are going to see a family counselor as well to work on our relationship. We mean so much to each other, and we love both of you as well. I love you very much.

Love,
Mom

September 6, 2009

Dear girls,

More than two thousand friends and former classmates of Jaycee Dugard held a parade in her honor in her hometown of South Lake Tahoe, California, on Sunday. Dugard was kidnapped while on her way to school in 1991.

South Lake Tahoe Celebrates Jaycee Dugard's Return with Pink Ribbon Parade

September 6, 2009

South Lake Tahoe celebrated the life of Jaycee Lee Dugard on Sunday under a canopy of 1,000 hot pink balloons.

The Pink Ribbon Parade, sponsored by Soroptimist International of South Lake Tahoe, drew about 2,000 people, South Lake Tahoe Police Chief Terry Daniels said.

"I wasn't surprised," Daniels said. "The community has been very supportive.... Everyone was excited anticipating this."

Sunday's parade traveled from the South Lake Tahoe Branch of the El Dorado County Library on Rufus Allen Boulevard to South Lake Tahoe Middle School, the reverse of the route a Soroptimist commemorative parade took in 2001, the 10th anniversary of Dugard's kidnapping, when she was 11 years old.

Dugard was found alive in Northern California in August, 18 years after her abduction. Phillip Craig Garrido, 58, and his wife, Nancy, 55, are being held in the case.

"It's signifying a full circle," Soroptomist Sue Novasel said of the parade.

Marchers came from throughout the area and included people who had lived in the area when Dugard was abducted, some who had attended school with her and people who had heard the story and wanted to show their support for Dugard, her friends, and family.

"We wanted to celebrate and rejoice," said Kelly Tousey of Fair Oaks, Calif., who attended the event with her family. She and her husband have three children, ages 5, 14 and 16.

"We have to watch over them very, very closely," Chris Tousey said. (www.rgj.com/story/news/2014/04/06/south-lake-tahoe-celebrates-jaycee-dugards-return-with-pink-ribbon-parade/7182977/)

September 30, 2009

Dear Kendall,

We took you to the Recreation Center for the first week of the month.

Monday	Tuesday	Wednesday	Thursday	Friday
Off with Dad	El Dorado Beach	Water games Climbing wall	Surprise Day	Movie Swim

School started so late this year that you started a week later than normal for this time of year. You usually start school the day after Labor Day, which is normally the first weekend, but you started the second week of the month. We found out before you started class that you did not get Ms. Hood as a teacher this year. You were so bummed. You had her for two years, and this year, she was stuck with teaching only first grade instead of a first/second combo class.

The teacher's name on the roster said Henderson. We didn't know if your teacher was male or female. You came home after the first day of school and told us that your teacher was Mr. Henderson. This is the first male teacher you have ever had. You really like him too. He is teaching a second/third combo class, and there are only five second graders in the class out of eighteen. You were nervous but walked right into class and sat down next to your friend McKenna. You mentioned that Mr. Henderson is funny and that you do these silly little dances in class. You even said that you wish he will be your teacher again next year.

Back to school night was two days after school started. It seemed so sudden to have that already, but we went to meet your teacher and see what he was going to do this year. He seems very nice, and he's coming in fresh to the school. This is his first year teaching up here.

We have decided that you are old enough to start taking showers instead of baths. You usually get in the shower first, and then Kasi will get in with you, and you help her get clean. It really helps us out and saves our backs from leaning over the tub. I got you each a little foam scrubby so that it is easier for you to scrub soap on your bodies.

The Fishing Derby was at Tahoe Paradise Park this year. We went fishing for free. We didn't catch anything this year. We had trouble with our bait this time. We did win a prize from a raffle though. You won a snowboard video game that you plug into the TV. It came with a little board that you stand on. You are both hot doggers with it now. You spin around on it and fall off every now and then.

We went to the fall festival at the college. We took pictures of you guys in the scarecrow stand. You even watched a puppet show about bears and trash. It was cute.

Soccer has been a challenge this season. We have had some tough teams that we are playing against. I decided to set up a practice with the fathers and daughters. This was a challenge as well because the dads had not signed up as volunteers, so the dads could only play against their own daughters or to the other dads. This was also good for the girls because they, too, could only play against their own dads or the other girls. They basically had to follow their dads around the field. It was a great turnout as well as a great practice. Both the dads and the girls really enjoyed themselves. It was a good bonding time too. It has been fun coaching your team.

Aunt Lucy and Cousin Denise came to Tahoe for a wedding, and it just so happens that we were able to meet up with them. Aunt Lucy is Mommy's aunt from Grandpa's side. Denise is her daughter. I hadn't seen Lucy for about twenty years, and I had never met Denise until this trip. We went to dinner with them one night when they were here, and then we went to the pool at the hotel they were staying at. We have so much more family that we haven't even seen or met. It was nice to spend time with them.

I love you.

Love,
Mom

October 31, 2009

Dear Kendall,

You had your walkathon this month. This year, both Daddy and I volunteered our time to help. I oversaw tally marking for all the girls in the class. You did forty-three laps, and the highest in the class was Ashley with sixty-three laps. You even walked a lap with Mr. Henderson, holding his hand.

You went on a field trip with your class to the farmer's market. You brought back a pumpkin, an ear of corn, and an apple. You had fun!

Our last soccer game, we played against the toughest team of the season. I was a little nervous because the first game we played against them, they pretty much kicked our butts. They play hard. I set up the game so that we were better prepared. We did not score as many goals as them in our last game, but we sure did give them a challenge. You girls did great! I was proud of you all.

We had a pizza party the following day to hand out awards and trophies. I made everyone a little certificate and gave all of you a pumpkin.

You went on another field trip to Apple Hill. We sent you with some money to be able to buy something while you were down there. You came back with an apple dessert to share with the family. That was very thoughtful of you.

You lost another tooth. I am almost wondering if you have any more teeth to lose. The tooth fairy left you a dollar for your tooth. I want to say that you saved your dollar and spent it on books at your book fair at school.

Daddy and I went to your parent/teacher conference with Mr. Henderson. He said that you were doing very well in class except for you talk a lot, but he said that all of you are talking a lot in class, so nothing major to report. He said that your test scores look good. They are a little lower than last year, but that was normal for the first trimester. Summer vacation sets kids back a little for when they start up again. He mentioned that most of your work will be English and math and that you will take the state test this year for the first time. You will be learning most of your subjects at a second-grade level, but your science and social studies will be at third grade level.

We carved pumpkins with Grandma. Kasi didn't want to put her hand in the pumpkin because it didn't look good, and it felt slimy. You were all into it. You love slimy stuff. You wanted to do a vampire pumpkin, and Kasi wanted to do a ghost on hers.

We went out to try and get a family photo with all the colors of fall in the background. I thought there were going to be some more reds, but there were more yellow and orange trees. We got a few good photos though.

Halloween turned out to be a very off day for us. We were supposed to start off the day with Kasi's Harvest Festival at her school, but we missed it. We were supposed to go to Kendall's Halloween Carnival at her school, but we missed that too. We ended up starting later than we had planned. Kasi was invited to her friend's birthday, so we started there. Then we went to the Horizon Casino. They had put together a little carnival and game area for the kids inside a convention center room. From there, we went to Kahle Community Center. Our last stop was Treat Street at the Pinecone Lodge. By the time we got you both over to Grandma's house, you were tired yet bouncing off the wall because of all the candy. I was glad it was over.

This year, you were a witch. Kasi was Scooby-Doo again. I put makeup on both of you. I made your eyes darker and painted a nose on Kasi. I dressed up as a pirate. It was fun!

I love you.

Love,
Mom

November 17, 2009

Dear girls,

I have some very sad news for you both. The infant room teacher, Teo Yelle, died last Thursday. She originally went to see the doctor because she had a cold. She was getting worse within a weeks' time. Once at the doctor's office, they informed her that she had pneumonia. Apparently bad too. They induced her into a coma, meaning a deep sleep or unconsciousness. They flew her to Reno and placed her into the intensive care unit. She had a few strokes, and her kidneys started to shut down while she was there. She had appeared to be getting better a day or two later, but then she had another big stroke. Her brain was dying from all the malfunctions happening in her body all at once. The doctor informed her family that she was pretty much brain dead from the stroke, and only about 30 percent of her brain was alive. They decided to take her off life support, and she didn't make it. She had died.

Teo was an amazing person! Mommy used to work with Teo in the baby room at the CDC. We were the "calm" after the storm. The babies would be loud and fussy when we arrived at the school. Once the two of us walked in and took over; the room had a more relaxed feeling. We were a great team together and were very similar in style when it came to caring for the babies. We treated them as one of our own. Teo still had something special about her when it came to the babies, a gift. A heart like no other.

Teo used to be Kasi's infant teacher when she was three months old. I had a hard time going back to work and leaving her, but I knew that she would be just fine. Kasi loved going to school and seeing Teo. She didn't cry when I dropped her off or picked her up. When I would pick her up, she was always in a good mood and happy.

Teo is loved by many babies and their families. She has watched over many children over the years, and most of the babies end up attached to her. The babies would cry when she walked out of the room and they could not see her.

There was a display wall in the front of the CDC for people to write things about Teo to post on the wall. Kasi wrote, "I'm telling God to take care of her." "I miss Teo!" Kendall wrote. "Teo was a good person, and she was a good teacher and she was helpful and she was nice."

I asked you both if you remembered who Teo was. Kasi said that she was in the hospital, and she was very sick. I told you that she did not make it out of the hospital and that she got very sick. She ended up dying in the hospital. You were both very quiet in the car for a couple minutes, and then Kasi said, "Mommy, that's not funny." I told you that I was not trying to be funny and that it is very sad that we will never see her again. It has been very hard for the families at the CDC.

There has been talk about naming the infant room after her. We all will miss her deeply. She was one of a kind.

Love,
Mom

November 29, 2009

Dear Kendall,

Each school had signed up to decorate a tree to auction them off. Each class at your school made an ornament. For your class, it was snowflakes. I signed up to help make ornaments with your class. It was very messy but very cute.

Kasi finally decided to cut her hair. Daddy has been bugging us to get her hair cut since she was about two years old. I kept telling him no. I told him that she would decide when she'd want your hair cut. She said that she wanted it like sissy's. Which was a little below her shoulders. It turned out cute. She liked it too. Daddy was so happy. You and Kasi look more alike now because your hair is the same.

You had a sleepover at your friend McKenna's house, and Kasi wanted to have a sleepover, but she had school the next day, and you didn't. She didn't even want to stay home with me. She asked to go to Grandma's house since you were going to someone else's house. You both crack me up. You fight when you are together, but when you're not together, you miss each other.

Auntie Mandy and her friend Kevin came to visit us. The last time Auntie Mandy was here was when Kasi was born. She brought you and Kasi a present. They came over to our house for dinner one night. You and Kevin hit it off great. Kevin helped you with your homework, and you became buds. They were here for about a week for Kevin's birthday. Auntie Mandy is Mommy's best friend from school. She lives in Portland, Oregon. I really miss her being closer to us.

Kasi had her first playdate with Tinley. Tinley came over to our house to play with her. She was excited about her coming over. You all three played upstairs in your room and watched a little *SpongeBob*.

The following weekend, she had her first sleepover at Tinley's house. She made it through the whole night without getting scared. She had a great time. I was so proud of her. She made it seem as though she'd done it before. You, on the other hand, had a hard time with sissy having a playdate and you didn't. I think you missed her.

You were having a feast and singing a song at your school for Thanksgiving, but I couldn't make it to both yours and Kasi's. Your school is farther away, and I could only go to one of them. Daddy was trying to go to both, but they were at the same time, and he went to yours first. By the time he got to her school, it was over. So we each went to one of your feasts at your schools.

We had Thanksgiving with Uncle Jeff and Auntie Tina at their house. It was fun and relaxing. You both play with the boy toys they have from Bobby and Travis. Grandma went to her friend Annie's house, and Grandpa was not feeling well, so he stayed home.

I love you very much.

Love,
Mom

December 12, 2009

Dear friends and family,

We are coming to an end of a very challenging year. I am hoping that the next year will be a better one for sure. With the economy and lack of jobs, it is hurting our town a lot. Many changes are coming and going. We are ready for good things to come our way. We did have fun along the way no less this year!

Art took the girls to the Father/Daughter Dance they have here every year. This was Kasi's first year to go. They were both so excited. They had a great time and saw a lot of their friends there as well.

Kendall played three sports this year—basketball, baseball, and soccer. She likes basketball and is pretty good at it. She was the only girl in an all-boys league. She can stand her ground though. Baseball was a first this year, and she wasn't really into it. Again, she was the only girl on an all-boys team. I don't think it's the sport for her. It's not active enough for her. Although her coaches said that she was great and should play on an older team. Soccer is her all-time favorite. We had a great season. She was the hot dog player on the team.

Kasi played soccer for the first time this year. I coached both of their teams. She had fun. She can't wait until the next season starts already.

We went to Disneyland for their birthdays this year. We didn't even tell them we were going. We stayed at Art's sister's house for one night then said it was crowded and that we were going to a hotel. We didn't tell them until we walked through the gates and saw Mickey's head on the lawn. It was so much fun. It was the best vacation ever! Now they ask us when we are going to Disneyland again. I think their favorite ride was Splash Mountain. Kasi got her favorite characters from the movie *Toy Story*. They sleep with her in her bed. They both had their pictures taken with a lot of the characters in the parks as well. Kendall went on all the big kid rides. She loved California Screamin', a large roller coaster in California Adventure.

Kasi had two performances at her school this year. One was for Multicultural Day, and they sang "It's a Small World After All." Funny how we just got back from Disneyland too. The other one was for their little graduation they have every year for the kids that are moving on to kindergarten. She still has one more year of preschool to go though.

Kendall had a visit to the emergency this summer. She was playing on the monkey bars at a summer camp, slipped, and hit her head on the frame of the bars. The ambulance came to get her and wrapped her up on the board with a neck brace. I think this park scared her more than the fall. She didn't hurt anything, but she sure gave me some gray hair. She's a little cautious on the monkey bars now though. I think it really scared her.

Kendall started second grade this year. She is in a second/third grade combo class. There are eighteen students, five of which are second graders. She is one of them. This will be her first male teacher. She loves him though. She's hoping that she has him again next year. She is doing well in school. Math is her favorite subject.

Halloween was a very business day for us. We went to six different events that day. Kendall was a witch this year, and Kasi was Scooby-Doo.

Kasi had her very first sleepover with a friend from school. She's only four years old and walked out the door without saying goodbye. She had her sleepover bag packed and ready to go as soon as she woke up. She made it through the night too.

Other fun things we did—kayaking, swimming at the beach, water parks, horseback riding, gymnastics, played miniature golf, watched fireworks, ice-skating, climbed on climbing walls, bike riding, play tennis, hiking, fishing, went to the movies, Shakespeare Theatre, went to museums, sledding, and made snowmen.

Art received his bachelor's in behavioral sciences this summer. He is planning on starting his master's degree in the fall through the University of San Francisco. I don't know if he will ever finish school. I think he just wants to be a permanent student. He's going for a master's in psychology and counseling.

I'm doing better now. I lost thirty pounds, and I'm trying to stay healthier. I would still like to lose about another ten to fifteen more though. I'm still working for the County of Education handling the enrollment for preschools. I have been there two years now. Other than that, I'm still pluggin' away at being Mom.

I hope you all have a Merry Christmas and a Happy New Year.

Love always,
Jeanna, Art, Kendall, and Kasi

December 31, 2009

Dear Kendall,

We went to the annual pancake breakfast with Santa. This year, you told Santa that you wanted Heelys again. I've been trying to discourage you from asking for these because I feel they are too dangerous, but that's what you asked for.

You went Christmas shopping at your school. It was called the Jingle Bell Shop. This is where you were able to pick out and buy gifts yourself for the family. You bought me a pretty necklace, earrings, and a teddy bear holding a rose. For Daddy, you picked out a green ornament that says "Dad" on it. Grandma got the same ornament, only it was purple and said "Grandma" on it. Grandpa you bought a little notepad that says, "Grandpa #1." You said that you wanted to get him a pad of paper with his name on it because Kasi always takes his pad of paper. For Kasi, you wanted to get her a bear that had "sister" on the shirt, but it was more money than you could spend. Uncle Jeff, you bought a key light, and Auntie Tina, you bought a teddy bear holding a rose. You were so excited when you came home that you made us all open our presents instead of waiting until Christmas. You even bought yourself some pencils, and a couple of your friends bought you a couple of things. You did chores to earn money to spend on your shopping spree.

The Festival of Trees and Lights was an event that is new this year that Barton Hospital Foundation put together. We didn't go to all the events that were planned because they were too expensive, but we did go to the main event. There were Christmas trees everywhere. Each one is decorated by a company or group. They were being auctioned off. Your school made ornaments for a tree, and it, too, was auctioned off. We saw your ornament on the tree. Your class made snowflakes that I helped your class make. Your tree also won Best of Show out of over twenty trees from Santa Claus's vote.

There was a fundraiser at Chevy's Restaurant for Teo Yelle's family. There was a lot of support from families of the CDC. It was like a preschool reunion. All of Kasi's friends showed up, and she was so excited to see her friends at the restaurant. I think the support of all the families that helped with the fundraiser, the total amount of support we gave them was about $1,000. It was very touching to see all the support. Her husband and daughter showed up right after we left. They were very grateful for the support.

Santa called our house. He talked to Kasi first. Then he asked what you wanted for Christmas. You told him that you wanted Heelys. He asked you if there was something else you might want since the snow was on the ground outside, you wouldn't be able to wear them. You didn't say much after that.

Horizon Casino put together an event for Christmas this year called the Candy Cane Lane. It was all decorated with candy canes and a gingerbread house. You and sissy made a gingerbread house together. You made some ornaments and decorated cookies as well. You sat on Santa's lap and took pictures. You told him you wanted Heelys again. I think he keeps asking you just in case you change your mind. You also wrote him a letter and mailed it off. There was a drawing, and Grandma won a gift card for $20 to the arcade. You both wanted to go to the arcade right then.

We saw Santa a few more times this month as well. We went to the Tahoe Keys to see Santa, and you got goody bags from him and a stocking. We went to Ernie's Coffee Shop, and you received an ornament, a cookie, and some hot chocolate.

We spent Christmas Eve at Uncle Jeff and Auntie Tina's house. Travis was up visiting, and he brought his Wii with him. We had dinner at their house. You and Kendall played the Wii for hours while we were over there. You both like swordplay, table tennis, bowling, cycling, golf, basketball, and more.

Christmas morning, you both woke up early, of course. We put together everything in bags and went to Grandma and Grandpa's house to open presents and have breakfast with Grandpa before he went to work. You were so excited to find out that Grandpa ended up getting you both little SpongeBob skateboards. Santa left you and sissy a Wii. You both wanted to play it right away. I had to figure out how to hook it up on Grandma's TV. You also got new tights, little gloves, electric toothbrushes, your own gum, a pair of reindeer earrings, a "Guess Who?" board game, a "Wheel of Fortune" board game, Fur Real Friends, and High School Musical Barbie doll. Grandpa bought us a new DVD player, Snuggies (blankets), and more ornaments for the tree. Even Chili dog got a new sweater.

You both had to brush your teeth with your new electric toothbrushes right after you opened all your presents. You both ask me for gum when I pick you up from school, so I got you each your own pack of gum. The "Wheel of Fortune" game is for Grandma, but you girls watch the show with her, so I'm sure that you will play it at Grandma's house more than ours. You and sissy both rolled around in the kitchen on your skateboards. You both played the Wii for about five hours on Christmas morning.

I think you had a pretty good Christmas. You were happy with the things that you got.

Aunt Carol and Uncle Lowell sent you and sissy books for Christmas. Yours was *Cinderella*. We sent thank you cards to them. You drew a picture for them to say thank you.

Santa wrote back two letters, one from the event at the Festival of Trees and Lights and the other from the Candy Cane Lane event. It was nice of him to write you two letters even though he's been very busy with all the kids he sees. You even got one of your letters printed in the newspaper.

You and Daddy built a snow cave in the front yard.

Your cousins—Marco Polo, Chela, Polito, Chelita, Andres, and Aaron—came to visit us. We went sledding with them in the snow. A couple of us went over some bumps and hurt our butts though.

For New Year's Day, we spent the evening over at your friends Devin and Olive's house with a group of people, and we celebrated the New Year in New York time so that we could celebrate it early for all the kids. We danced and laughed a lot.

Happy New Year, baby girl. I love you.

Love,
Mom

About the Author

 Jeanna Rangel was born and raised in South Lake Tahoe, California. She was an only child raised by her mother. Her father wasn't in the picture much, so it was a difficult childhood. She was a very determined individual and grew up quickly. Jeanna attended college at the University of Southern California. She originally wanted to be an animator, but without the experience, she found it very hard to find a job after graduating. She finally decided that she was not a city girl, and her debt was growing. She moved home. She decided to get married and start a family. She had two beautiful girls that she devoted her life to, and she was determined to give them a better life than she had. No matter how hard you try to be the best parent, ultimately, your children grow and decide for themselves who they want to be. She lives about two blocks away from her girls, but they are still learning and making their way through life. Still with a little help from Mom, of course.

Printed in the USA
CPSIA information can be obtained
at www.ICGtesting.com
LVHW092142301124
797921LV00002B/142